STOP BEING STUPID

Your Adventure from Victimhood to Radical Self-Love

CAROL WIRTH

Saul to Paul
PUBLISHING

You may contact the publisher at:
Saul to Paul LLC
www.SaultoPaulllc.com
SaultoPaul@gmail.com

Cover Designer: Heather Wilbur
Photo Credit LDJ Photography
Interior Design Credit: Woven Red Author Services, www.WovenRed.ca

Stop Being Stupid/Carol Wirth—1st edition
ISBN: 978-0-692-70927-6

Dear Reader,

I want to share how this book came to be- the story of its genesis and completion. What you will read is really a demonstration of the work I have asked you to take on in "Stop Being Stupid."

I was a successful high school teacher for 26 years. Teaching was an exciting and fulfilling profession for me. Most especially I loved watching students learn for themselves how capable they were. And yet, as much as I enjoyed watching the wonder of self discovery I knew that I had a gift inside of me that was not being delivered. Something in me was speaking to me, and had been for years.

In March of 2015 I said yes to the gift. I said yes to God/Spirit. I said yes to myself. I asked for guidance. I wasn't quite sure what was about to happen. What's next? I resigned my tenured teaching position, moved out of the house I had grown to love and moved to a cabin on Priest Lake, Idaho for the summer.

At that time I had no clear picture what to do next. I knew I was to write a book and, on a wider scale, teach the inner work I had been teaching on an individual basis for years. But how?

I spent hours day after day in prayer, meditation, studying sacred text, in contemplation, and communion with God/Spirit. I walked, biked and ran the forest trails. I kayaked and frolicked, played the piano and played and played. I rested, and listened to music and talks by Reverend Maggie Buck and Reverend Michael Beckwith. I danced, I sang, I cooked, I traveled and went on my yearly "Agape Soul Sisters Retreat." I played some more.

And then, I began to write. The first draft came in about a three-week period. It came through me. I asked for help with what to do next. Help came in the form of editors, a website designer/marketer, and publishing professionals. Seemingly, out of nowhere, the right people showed up at the right time with the expertise I needed.

Guidance is a principle. It is always available and I was asking continuously, and so I received guidance step by step. In fact it has become my way of life.

"Stop Being Stupid" is the result of my going with the flow and continuing to do the work necessary to come from my authentic Radical Self-Love, Child of God Identity. Following what I was hearing took a willingness to do the next obvious thing, and then the next obvious thing, and then the next obvious thing again, one day at a time even when I wanted to give up. Trusting God/Spirit is simple, but not always easy.

The entire process from start to finish took a total of approximately nine months. Right. Just like a baby. Well I suppose "Stop Being Stupid" is my "baby," because just like a child, this book came through me but in truth came from God/Spirit. And just like a child I have no idea where it will end up, nor what its impact may be.

Thus, if this book is helpful to you in any way, know that it is God/Spirit's gift to you.

Peace, Blessings and Love to you!
Carol Wirth

This book is dedicated to Pat and Mike Wirth, my parents.
Thank you for teaching me to include, love and appreciate all people.
I love you!

Table of Contents

Acknowledgments...13

How Dare You! An Introduction I

Chapter 1: Why was I so miserable? 1

    A Tiny Drop of Sewage 4
    Chapter 1 Summary 6

Chapter 2: Are you a card-carrying member of the "Hood"? 7

    What's really going on here? Who am I? And who are you?.................9
    Who's doing it to you now?..16
    Excuse me, but how much does that Victim Identity cost? 18
        What's it costing you? 19
        What's the pay off? 21

    Chapter 2 Summary 23

Chapter 3: Pre-Requisites for Transformation...............25

    Are you ready to drop the Blame Game?....................25
    How do I transform?..28
    Chapter 3 Summary 33

Chapter 4: How do I know when I'm adding a Drop of Sewage? 34

    Being aware of Patterns..34
    The Usual Suspects and Their Alias' (AKA) (Also Known As) 36
        People Pleasing: (AKA: The Chameleon/Narcissist) 36
        Manipulation and Control: (AKA: The Control Freak!).....37
        Caretaking/Rescuing: (AKA: The Super Hero) 38

Hyper-responsibility (AKA: It's my fault!)....................................39
Poll-taking (AKA: Waffling and Indecisiveness) 40
Busyness: (AKA: The Squirrel)..40
Complaining, Judging and Blaming: (AKA: The Perfectionist) 41
Self-Neglect and Destructive Behaviors: (AKA: The Martyr)...................42
Hypersensitivity: (AKA: The Drama Queen or King)............................43
Combativeness: (AKA: Screw you! You're not the boss of me!) 44
A word about Addictions 45
Wishful Thinking: (AKA: Fantasy Land Diary)....................................46
Resignation and Detachment: (AKA: Screw it) 47

Chapter 4 Summary 48

CHAPTER 5: NOW THAT I CAN SEE THE DROP OF SEWAGE, HOW DO I STOP ADDING IT TO MY GLASS? 51

You are the sewage broker in your life 52
Are you ready to stop Pimp'n your Soul?......................................53
Chapter 5 Summary 55

CHAPTER 6: FREEDOM AIN'T FREE! 57

What's it gonna take to Radically Love You? 59
Radically Loving You: The Short Cut 60
Cultivating a relationship with God/Spirit and stepping into your
Authentic Radical Self-Love, Child of God Identity 61
How DO I Love Myself Radically? 62
Higher Power Anyone? 64
Design a God/Spirit 67
    Affirmations 71

Chapter 6 Summary 72

CHAPTER 7: UNDERSTANDING AND APPLYING SPIRITUAL LAW- WORD! 74

Gravity is 76
Hit me! Are you asking for it?...77
Looking for Demonstrations 77

The Laws- Line Up! 79
Spiritual Law- Get in Align! 80
   The Law of Life 80
   The Law of Mind in Action or the Law of Experience 80
   The Law of Karma 81
   The Law of Multiplicity 82
   The Law of Focus 82
   The Law of Asking 83
   The Law of Opposites 84
   The Law of Gratitude and Appreciation 85
   The Law of Flow and Resistance 87
   The Law of It's All Good 88

An Exceedingly Dark Time 90
Chapter 7 Summary 96

CHAPTER 8: PRACTICING THE PRESENCE AND TRAINING YOUR THINKING 97

The Only Way you Coast is Down Hill 97
Practice, Practice, Practice 99
   Morning and/or Evening Spiritual Practice 99
   Prayer 100
   Gratitude 101
   Music 101
   Inspirational Reading 101
   Additional Journaling 102
   Meditation 103
   Morning Intentions 104
   Coffee Walk 107
   Evening Forgiveness Ritual 107
   Evening Intentions 108
   Evening Questions 108
   Empowering Questions 109
   Disempowering Questions 109

Training Your Thinking 111
   Upsets that Pass 112
   Upsets that Last 113
   Drop it! 114

Leave it! 114

Come! 115

Stay! 115

Fetch! 115

You Have Dominion 115

Drop it! 117

Leave it! 118

Stay! 119

Fetch! 119

No Barking! 120

Chapter 8 Summary 120

CHAPTER 9: I'M NOT BUYING A FUCKING TEDDY BEAR! — WHEN UPSETS WON'T BUDGE 122

Inner Child Work 122

Now it's Your Turn 125

Purging 126

Steps for a Purge 127

Venting 128

Steps for a Venting 129

Forgiveness 129

Forgiveness Steps for Stubborn Resentments or Hurts 131

Clean-up 132

Resistance 133

I don't wanna! 134

They might not want you to either! 135

Is this a Boundaries Issue? 136

Chapter 9 Summary 138

CHAPTER 10: ARE YOU YOUR OWN BEST FRIEND YET? 140

Radically Self-Loving Practices 141

Exercise 142

Proper Nutrition 142

Good Hygiene and Good Sleep Hygiene 143

Dating Yourself: Celebrate You! 143
Spending time in Nature 144
Music and Art 145
Mirror Work 145
Self Hugging, and the Thymus Thump 146
EFT (Emotional Freedom Techniques) 146
Laughter Makes for Good Medicine 148
On-going Forgiveness Ritual. "Up until now..." 148
Hugging and Smiling 150
Gratitude and Appreciation 150

Chapter 10 Summary 152

CHAPTER 11: THIS IS A GOOD BEGINNING! PAY IT FORWARD! ..154

It's a We-thing! 158
Onward! 158
Community 159
Chapter 11 Summary 160

ABOUT THE AUTHOR 163

READING GROUP GUIDE 165

ACKNOWLEDGMENTS

I want to thank the many teachers, guides and mentors who have helped me on this journey. They are: Charles Singleton, Reverend Maggie Buck, Tyrone Jackson, Reverend Michael Bernard Beckwith, Debbie Lyons, Barbara Williams, Rickie Byars Beckwith, Hedi Hesse, and Wells Wetherell. Without the help of these wise ones, I would not have survived my life while being stupid. I love you all!

My content editors were straight and insightful with their feedback. They are Dave Bauer, Jodana Campbell, Bob Scarfo, Kirsten Saxton and Nicole Lang. My line editor Kirsten Saxton thankfully caught and corrected grievous and annoying grammar and punctuation errors. My beta readers was Bob Scarfo who, with his super power vision, caught all of the invisible errors. I love you all!

Lucina Jacowich shot the cover photo, and Heather Wilbur designed the cover in just the right way. Joan Leacott formatted the book with the patience of a saint. Jennifer Gatts is the fabulous website and marketing Guru extraordinaire! And the brilliant JD DeWitt put it all together and is the Head Cheese in charge of distribution. I love you all!

I also want to thank my family and friends for their unflagging support. I love you all!

Lastly I want to thank God/Spirit and the ancestors for lifting me up time and again when I wanted to quit. I love you!

How Dare You! An Introduction

"How dare you!" My niece teased me about this book's title.

I admit I had second thoughts about the title myself. I remember thinking, "Stop Being Stupid? Really? *That's the title?* Dear God Carol, it's so politically incorrect. Couldn't you say something more, well, positive?"

Hmmm... let's just say as Forest Gump would, *"Stupid is as stupid does."* By *that definition I was being stupid, and you might be too.*

Let me start by telling you about how I got here.

The year was 1996. I was 33 years old, over seven years away from using any alcohol or mind-altering drugs, and seven years into a successful career. I had a book being published by Viking-Penguin with my soon to be ex-husband; had an Adonis-like boy friend with whom I was madly in love; a new job in a school in Oakland, California that was a perfect fit for me. I was the thinnest I'd been in years; in the best physical shape of my life. And I was utterly and completely miserable. I was suicidal and homicidal.

All my ducks seemed to be perfectly well behaved, but there I was, once again, empty, depressed, angry and afraid. I was so sure it was my husband that had been the problem. I was sure that this time, with this new man, this new job, my renewed physical vitality and skinny body that I'd finally fixed myself.

I sat in a 12-step meeting crying, and in desperation I uttered a little prayer to a God I was sure had condemned me and was punishing me. I said *"Please God help me. I can't live like this anymore."* I remember nothing more about the meeting.

After the meeting I stood outside on the corner of East 14th and 47th Avenue in Oakland, a hard scrabbly spot that is arguably the least likely place for a miracle or an epiphany. I was tearfully complaining to some patient soul, when I felt a gentle hand on my shoulder. My soon to be spiritual mentor, Charles, looked me straight in the eye and said, *"I have no idea what you are talking about, and don't take this personally, but stop being stupid."*

The undeniable truth of that statement struck me silent. I felt like Moses in front of the burning bush getting my very own extra special 11th commandment. I started laughing; it was so simple. How many times had I heard it? Insanity is doing the same thing over and over and expecting different results. Insanity-or stupidity, I'm not sure why but it was easier for me to swallow being stupid.

Charles used to say to me, *"Carol, you're very intelligent, but not too smart."* He had me there.

"Stop being stupid." It sounds simple enough, doesn't it? Let's look at what that really means.

Stop *means to cause to give up, or cease or change a course of action.*

Stupid *means to be senseless, irrational or dull.*

So when I say *"Stop being stupid,"* I mean give up being senseless, irrational or dull, and change your course of action.

But how do you do that? How do you give up being senseless, and irrational when you've been doing it for years? And how do you even know what to stop and what course of action to take instead?

For all of my brothers and sisters who have followed in my same stupid footsteps, this book is for you.

Although you can't do it wrong, you can do it long. I have done it long and suffered greatly, and perhaps unnecessarily. I am writing this book in the hopes that it helps you to stop being stupid more quickly than I did.

Henry David Thoreau wrote, "*Most men lead lives of quiet desperation and go to the grave with the song still in them.*"

Now that's normal, isn't it? Most people don't live life to the fullest. Most people don't risk being authentic. We follow the herd. We believe that if we get enough accolades, achievements, and things we'll be happy; or we do what everyone else is doing, or get a little more than the next guy, we'll be happy.

By that standard, I was as normal as they come and it left me miserable, empty and desperate.

This book is about transformation, Radical Self-Love and authenticity. It is about how to become abnormally happy, joyous and free. It is both a chronicle and a how-to guide for those interested in living life authentically and full out.

This process is an adventure. It is about the journey, not a destination.

The origin of the word **adventure** is advetus venire *meaning to arrive, to come, more to come.*

An **adventure** *is an undertaking involving danger and unknown risks, an exciting and remarkable experience, to cope with the new and unknown, to take a risk.*

A **journey** *is travel or passage from one place to another, to travel over or through, to move in a given direction or path, or progression.*

When you choose to take this adventure, this journey of *Radical Self-Love*, you can't know ahead of time how it's going to turn out. It is inherently risky to your normal life. There are no guarantees that you'll get what you think you want.

This adventure means traveling over and through your inner landscape always in the direction and on the path to *Radical Self-Love*. It involves coping with the unknown and arriving once again at *Radical Self-Love*, only to find that there is always more to come.

Every day is a new beginning! It is indeed an exciting and remarkable experience. It is worth the risk. It is worth risking a normal life that is predictable and safe and cluttered with all the material things you thought would bring happiness.

For those who are "*sick and tired of being sick and tired,*" this book can offer hope and help. I will share with you my adventure and journey, and provide you detailed instructions for the practices that have given me back my life and awakened me to my Authentic Self.

For the record, there is nothing that I will say here that hasn't been said before. The truths that I share have been taught for centuries in different formats. The only thing that is unique is my individual expression of these truths. My discovery of them and the adventure/journey of that process are the story of how I came to remember my Authentic Identity.

I am singing the song that I have discovered within me- the song that I must sing. My purpose in writing this book is to be of service to *God/Spirit* and to you.

My intention for you is that reading about my journey and doing the work suggested will help you recognize the truth of what you are-the hidden splendor within you. What you are, as a human being, is *Love*. That never changes, and we are all the same "what." But *who* you are is a unique ever-expanding individualized expression of the what.

I want you to discover and sing your song!

You will notice that repetitive themes run throughout the book, and critical information is repeated. This is by design. It sometimes takes hearing the same things several ways for it to make the two-foot drop- from head to heart- from knowing about something intellectually, to knowing it in your heart and soul.

I include the definitions of many key terms in the body of the text. It is often helpful to take a fresh look at what we think we already know to gain new insights.

If you have never done any inner or self-reflective work, I suggest that you read the book through once before doing the writing exercises. It is beneficial to get the big picture of these foundational ideas first.

This journey is yours. Welcome aboard.

You may not yet understand or believe what I am about to say. I want you to know that I wrote this book because I love you. It is my way of thanking you for loving me.

Peace and Blessings!
Carol Wirth
www.SaultoPaulLLC.com

STOP BEING STUPID

Chapter 1
Why was I so miserable?

"If you're going through hell, keep going."
– Winston Churchill

"If you're going through hell, don't pitch a tent!"
– Reverend Michael Bernard Beckwith

Despite my misery, my life while being stupid was working really well in many ways. Although I had moments of profound happiness, satisfaction and connection with people, I couldn't sustain it. In fact, most of the time I was ill at ease and slightly or completely depressed. There was a low level malaise and dissatisfaction that continued to resurface despite all the things I achieved that I thought would create happiness.

In our society that kind of depression is fairly common, hence the proliferation of antidepressants and other mood enhancing chemicals. It's normal.

So what was the basic cause of my misery?

My dominant unconscious belief was that I was a victim.

I believed that I had no real choices in life.

Again, this is a normal core belief, and business as usual for many people. Victimhood as an identity is normal, usual and ordinary.

Let's look at what that word actually means.

Victimhood *is the state or condition of being a victim.*

A **victim** *is one that is injured, destroyed or sacrificed, one who is subject to oppression, hardship or mistreatment, or one that is tricked or duped.*

The fact is, some very traumatic and horrible events occurred during my childhood about which I truly had no say. I was, in fact victimized.

Traumatic things happened to me. Perhaps if I had received counseling or therapy at the time, I'd have worked through the trauma and moved on, but I didn't. Instead I stayed rooted in a victim mentality that solidified into a false identity- the victim identity, or victimhood.

From the victim identity, I had no access to Self-Love, never mind *Radical Self-Love.*

I developed a belief that conditions, circumstances, heredity and past events would always call the shots in my life- and they did, because I made sure of it.

I used my experience to validate the belief that I was a victim. I had lots of evidence to prove that I was right, and I was always right about what I saw about the conditions of my own life, or so I thought.

From an early age, I knew I was different. I was sure there was something very wrong with me. I just didn't fit in anywhere. In my view the problem was that I was defective. I wanted to fix it, fix me.

But beyond a vague sense that I was undeniably bad, maybe even evil I didn't know what was wrong with me. I believed that I didn't have enough of the *"right things"* and/or had too much of the *"wrong things"* to ever really fit in with other people. I never experienced myself as being acceptable just as I was.

Thus, my earliest obsession was to fit in, or rather, appear to fit in. If I could fake it well enough or if I could do enough for the right people, at the right time; or if I saved or inspired enough people; or if someone loved me enough; then maybe, just maybe, I'd be good enough.

I wanted to be redeemed. I kept trying to figure it out. But, no matter what I did, it was never enough, because I wasn't enough. I believe that I would never be worthy. I never felt loved.

I was sure there was something outside of me that would allow me to feel OK with who I thought I was. I just needed to get the right thing, or have something done to me. I couldn't figure out what I was missing or where to get it. It was so confusing to be me.

I had developed the following constellation of beliefs:

- I don't fit in anywhere.
- No one will ever love me just the way I am.
- I'm not good enough.
- I don't deserve love, abundance, peace, joy etc.
- I'm bad, and I'm probably going to hell.
- I have to earn love, acceptance and respect.
- There's something wrong with me- I'm broken, damaged or missing something.
- People always use me and hurt me.
- People aren't safe, and you can't trust them.

I did whatever I thought was necessary to manipulate others to give me what I thought I needed to feel whole, and it never worked.

When I embraced the victim identity (victimhood) with the aforementioned constellation of beliefs, it was all about me- all of the time. I was completely self-absorbed and self-centered. Not that I thought very highly of myself, I didn't; but I thought *about* myself all of the time.

My particular flavor of victimhood was to model for you what I wanted with the understanding that you, *"owed it to me,"* to reciprocate.

I was kind and generous, or worked extra hours without pay, or did more than my share, or gave lavish gifts, or slept with you (if you were a man I was attracted to), or did favors, or supported any and every cause or person who asked. I was a great helper!

Sometimes I was clairvoyant. I could just tell you needed my help, especially if you didn't ask. My red cape was always cleaned and pressed, ready for action.

I was looking to earn being worthy. I just knew that someone was bound to notice how wonderful I was. Then, of course they'd give me an award or a prize, or love me enough or appreciate me or respect me enough to fix me. All of this kept me really, really, busy, and there was always a crisis or drama at hand.

I'd wait and wait, and when things didn't go the way I thought they should, or when I didn't like what was happening, I would get *"hurt feelings."* I'd feel angry, fearful, lonely, resentful, sad, jealous, envious, sorry for myself, or vengeful. I would say things like "*I feel abandoned, rejected, disrespected, wounded, unsafe, abused, fragile, neglected,*" none of which were actual feelings, but merely the **story** that I told about what I felt.

I believed those stories were proof that they were "*doing it to me,*" again. Sigh. I would get resigned, and dive into more self-pity. The cycle continued, feeding on itself. At some point I would buck up and do something else!

I'd do one of the following, I'd: run away, fight, or deny what was happening. These three strategies guaranteed that I would never actually face anything, nor take responsibility.

I had become a reactionary human-doing, control-freak, regularly chasing my own tail, and trying to herd people, places and things into just the right corral where they would stay put and make me happy. And I just couldn't do it anymore: the wheels where coming off.

A Tiny Drop of Sewage

"Is a tiny drop of sewage acceptable?"
– Tyrone Jackson

"Live full. Die Empty."
– Anonymous

Sheesh! You might be saying to yourself, glad I'm not like that! What a mess you were! True enough, but be clear, I wasn't operating from the victim identity one hundred percent of the time. I mean, hey my life was pretty good most of the time. I had a lot of good stuff going on, but... I was not satisfied.

See it's like this- Imagine your life is like a glass of your favorite beverage, really satisfying, refreshing- simply awesome. The victim identity, even if you come from it only occasionally is like adding a tiny drop of sewage to your glass: it taints the whole thing.

So here's a question to ponder: **Is a tiny drop of sewage acceptable?**

No, really, stop and answer the question for yourself.

Is it acceptable?

Let's get something really clear; sometimes people are victimized. People are hurt physically, emotionally, and mentally.

Abuse, neglect, murder, natural disasters, illness, and accidents all occur. Innocent victims are hurt or even killed.

No doubt.

I'm not saying they aren't.

However, there is a difference between working through the trauma of being a victim or even a perpetrator of traumatic experiences, and coming from a victim identity.

For most victims or perpetrators of trauma, the process of working through, accepting, letting go and forgiving is necessary. It allows people to move on and live a fulfilling life. When you don't complete that process it isn't healthy. You live with *"ghosts"* and keep repeating the victim or perpetrator drama. Living in that kind of drama is extremely detrimental.

When you take on the persona of a victim, you believe you are a victim of others (including *God/Spirit*), circumstances and even yourself. You are not free.

If you come from a victim identity even a fraction of the time, or only in certain areas of your life, it taints everything. It is a tiny drop of sewage in your wonderful glass of life. The beliefs and mentality of a victim begin to creep into all areas of life because it dictates who you are being.

Your way of being dictates what you do and how you do it. What you do determines what you have-your life experiences.

For example, one of my victim identity beliefs was that- *"People always use and hurt me."* That belief dictated that I "be" cautious, suspicious and tense. When I was being cautious, suspicious and tense everything seemed to be threatening and so my behavioral responses were defensive.

If I got a phone call, regardless of who was calling, (the power company, my work, or even a dear friend), my reaction would be the same. My first thought would be, *"What do they want from me now?"* If I answered the phone at all, I would be evasive, defensive and impatient. What I really wanted to say was *"Leave me alone!"* As you might guess those conversations were not enjoyable or productive.

Here's the thing, often as not, people were just calling to give me information, or see how I was doing, or invite me to do something, but I couldn't see that.

I could only see what the belief allowed *"People always use and hurt me."* It tainted my view, my perception. I only saw what I expected to see from that belief. That belief was a tiny drop of sewage; my vision was polluted.

CHAPTER 1 SUMMARY

- Believing you are a victim causes suffering.
- Believing you are a victim creates a false victim identity.
- The victim identity creates other false beliefs that lead to self-centered thoughts and actions that are disempowering.
- Coming from the victim identity is a way to avoid responsibility for one's life.
- Being victimized is not the same as coming from a victim identity.
- Coming from the victim identity is like adding a drop of sewage to your glass of life- it taints the whole thing.

Chapter 2
Are you a card-carrying member of the "*Hood*"?

You may be indulging in a victim identity if you:

1) Say yes when you want to say no and then blame the asker as if you had no choice.
2) Believe that in order to say no you have to have a *"good enough"* reason.
3) Believe other people can hurt your feelings.
4) Believe other people don't treat you right or can disrespect you.
5) Believe other people need to change for you to be happy.
6) Believe circumstances need to change for you to be happy.
7) Take the weather, traffic, politics, the economy or other people's behavior personally.
8) Believe other people's behavior means something about you.
9) Use the behavior of other people to either validate or invalidate yourself or what you are doing in life, or your dreams.
10) Resent others or hold grudges, or have *"justified"* ill will towards others.
11) Notice you have a lot of judgments about things or people, (including yourself)- but of course you're right!

12) Engage in name calling either openly, behind people's backs or in your head. (This also includes calling yourself names.)

13) Gossip and or complain about others, or yourself.

14) Have a hard time apologizing or refuse to admit that you are wrong or have made a mistake without justification.

15) Always have to be right, or have to let others know when they are wrong.

16) Beat yourself up when you make a mistake or don't know something, or for any other reason.

17) Are sure you would be happy if you just lost/gained weight, had a bigger or littler specific body part, were taller/shorter, darker/lighter, or in some way physically different.

18) Have either given up on your dreams, or have none.

19) Spend little or no time on your inner life, leisure, hobbies or play.

20) Are thinking to yourself that you don't really need to read this book, but boy do you know someone who should.

21) Were pissed off at the suggestion that any of the afore mentioned might indicate that you may be coming from a victim identity at times.

Hear what I am not saying.

I am not saying that you come from a victim identity at all times.

What I am saying is that when you experience life in any of the aforementioned ways, it is highly likely that the VICTIM Identity is in the house and running the show.

By the way, there's nothing wrong with that. We all get to choose.

However, it's no fun for you or anyone else in your life. No power, no peace, no freedom, no joy, no love, no genuine connection to your real Self, *God/Spirit* or others.

As I've heard it said, *"If you burn your ass, ya gotta sit on the blister."* Believing you are a victim is an ass burner.

The victim identity is all about being predictable. It is about creating predictably more of the same slow strangulating misery, and limping along until you die. The victim life is predictably dull, boring, sad, angst ridden, but safe.

It is safe and comfortable in a *"I know this misery"* kind of way. But is that what you really want?

Really?

Take a moment and answer that question for yourself. No one is looking at you. This is a *"To thine own self be true"* moment.

There is nothing wrong with choosing comfortable, safe misery; but it's not very satisfying.

There is an alternative, and you may not like it, because you can't have both. If you're anything like me, you might have to suffer longer to obtain sufficient motivation to finally turn your gaze inward rather than outward for your solution.

If you are willing to do this, you will have access to a new life.

New *means never before.*

A never-before life means that it is not predictable.

A never-before life means that business as usual won't work.

If you are unwilling to consider living life in a new way then throw this book away, or better yet give it to one of the people you are sure REALLY needs it.

WHAT'S REALLY GOING ON HERE? WHO AM I? AND WHO ARE YOU?

"Let it be done for you according to your faith."
– Matthew 9:29

"Someday, after we have mastered the winds, the waves, the tides and gravity, we shall harness...the energies of love.
Then, for the second time in the history of the world, we will have discovered fire.
– Pierre Tielhard de Chardin

There's nothing wrong with you.

Really.

There's nothing wrong with you.

You have merely misidentified yourself.

Anyone who is living a life devoid, consistently or intermittently, of peace, harmony, love, beauty, creativity, and abundance, is dealing with an *"identity* crisis," and is in fact, not dwelling in an authentic experience of *Radical Self-Love*.

Simply, you have forgotten what you really are and you have falsely identified yourself as a victim. You have forgotten that you have the power of Love within you. That it is what you are.

When you are in the victim identity, you think that you are your experiences, thoughts, mind, body, emotions, and feelings. You identify yourself with the things you own, what you do, and your achievements, titles or whom you are with. You are none of these and none of these things satisfy your soul.

When in the victim identity, I was looking for things, experiences and achievements to *"make"* me happy and satisfied. I disliked or even hated myself and I blamed circumstances, others and/or myself for my unhappiness and dissatisfaction.

For example, I was a teacher, and high school administrator for many years. I believed being an educator was a large part of my identity. I thought that if I was *"the best,"* then I'd be happy and satisfied.

When I completed a master's degree in educational leadership along with a Tier II administrative credential I felt a rush of satisfaction regarding that accomplishment. I became an administrator, and I can remember thinking, *"I've done it!"*

However, the elation was short lived and that achievement didn't really change the quality of my life. I even celebrated by taking a trip to Hawaii, but I only enjoyed parts of that trip. Ultimately, I was left feeling depressed and confused, and I can remember thinking, *"What am I doing wrong?"*

Let me break this down a little more. I can remember being shocked by the idea that I was not what I had experienced and achieved. But I was even more shocked by the notion that my body, thoughts and emotions were not the real me.

Let's see if you can experience the *"real you"* for a couple of minutes.

Stop for a moment. If possible find a quiet place to sit or lie down comfortably. If that's not possible, at least ask others not to disturb you for a few minutes.

Now, allow yourself to become physically still. Focus on your breath and simply observe your thoughts. It may help to close your eyes.

Become present to any emotions that arise and any body sensations that occur such as tenseness in your shoulders. Breathe in and out, and while you focus on your breath simply observe what goes on inside of you. Try this for a minute or two, or five if you are daring.

You may notice thoughts coming up like: *"This is stupid." "What's the point of this?" "I'm hungry. I really want that ice cream." "I'm sleepy." "That checker at the store was so slow."*

Allow yourself to just notice. Keep returning your attention to your breath. You may notice aches or discomfort in the body. You may feel peaceful, anxious, curious or sad. Allow yourself to simply notice it all. Do not attempt to alter anything. Simply observe.

Go ahead and try it now. I'll wait for you.

Now that you're back. What did you observe? What was going on inside of you while you sat still in the moment?

What was it that did the observing?

There is the *"you"* that had the experience of sitting, thinking, feeling, and the *"you"* that observed the *"you"* that had the experience.

The *"observer you,"* is the part of you that is not attached to the mind, thoughts, feelings, emotions or body. It is the non-physical, non-mental, non-emotional aspect of your self. It is the part of you that is directly connected to all of life. It is the changeless aspect of you, your being-ness. It is your soul, your essential *Self*, what I call *Radical Self Love, a Child of God*. It is your authentic identity.

It is that part of you that cannot be born, and will never die. It is life itself-the animating force. It is pure Love or Presence, or Life Energy. If you were to *"die"* that would be the part that was missing. It is the part that would leave the body.

But, you may say, what about my experiences and my achievements? They make me who I am, don't they? Nope. They are experiences by which we can learn and grow but they are not what or who you are.

You may experience a temporary sense of satisfaction or a high from acquiring certain things or having certain experiences, but the high does not last, and sometimes leaves you feeling disappointed and even more depressed.

It is who you are being in any given moment that determines your experience of life, whether you are peaceful and satisfied, or agitated and dissatisfied.

Again, what you are never changes, but who you are is up to you in any given moment.

"Let it be done for you **according to your** faith." Another way of saying that is, "*It is done unto you **AS** you believe.*" This statement is one of the most succinct descriptions of the Laws of Creation. It can also be stated this way: Think, Believe, Achieve.

Think a thought often enough and with enough emotion and you will begin to believe what you are thinking.

It doesn't really matter whether it is based on something that is true, or something that is false. If you think it enough, you will believe it.

Your beliefs cause you to see things in particular ways which creates your perceptions, or views.

Your perceptions dictate your ways of being in the world.

Your ways of being cause you to take particular actions.

Thus, you think, you believe, and you act accordingly. Therein lies the genesis of your created life.

And make no mistake about it; you are the creator of your life. You now have the opportunity to remember and embrace your authentic identity, and become a conscious co-creator of your life.

You see what you believe in your life, not the other way around.

You almost never see things as they really are.

Stop a moment and ponder that concept.

Life is like a mirror reflecting back to you who you are being based on what you believe.

You are so powerful in creating your life, that you can experience yourself as a victim, broken, defective, less than, unworthy, unlovable, unwanted, unsafe, or stupid.

On the other hand, you can experience yourself as loved, beautiful, wanted, needed, of priceless value, complete, whole, powerful, creative and magnificent!

When you come from the victim identity, even occasionally those victim drop-of-sewage beliefs leave you experiencing life in disempowering ways, and you act accordingly.

NO ONE IS DOING IT TO YOU. YOU ARE DOING IT TO YOURSELF.

This is great news!!!

As one of my friends, Milton used to say, *"If I'm not the problem, there is no solution."* Milton had two signs hanging on his bathroom mirror. At the top of the mirror was the phrase *"If I've got a problem,"* and at the bottom of the mirror was the phrase *"I'm looking at it."*

Touché Milton.

When I began this adventure I had no idea that I was coming from the false victim identity. I didn't know I had a choice.

I had problems with almost everyone and everything. If they would just change I could be happy!

Here are some examples of how I saw things in my life. See if you relate.

- My boyfriend lacked ambition and I had to motivate him.
- My students weren't working to their potential so I had to get them to be responsible and work harder.
- Some of my co-workers were incompetent, so I had to do way more than my share at work.
- My boxing coach was too demanding so I'd no choice but to be exhausted.
- My parents weren't taking care of their health the way they should, so I taught them to lift weights and make sure they were lifting. Bone density decreases with age don't you know!
- My friend wasn't paying back the money I loaned him, (I charged it on my high interest credit card!) so I had to harass him and constantly worry about paying that bill.
- I barely made enough money to pay the bills and it stressed me out!!!
- Gasoline prices were high and since I had to commute nearly an hour one way to my coach's gym, I had to rack up more credit card debt.
- My upstairs neighbor stomped around at night and so I had to be irritated and couldn't even feel relaxed at home!

You may notice my descriptions were saturated with the vocabulary and phrases of the victim identity: *had to; get them to; no choice; make sure they; it stressed me.*

I really believed these people, and circumstances, were causing me problems, and I had to react the way I did.

None of the people or circumstances caused a problem for me. Honestly, they didn't.

I finally saw that the one thing that all of these "problematic" people, situations and circumstances had in common was me.

I was the common denominator in all of my life problems. Both the problem and the solution were always a function of the way I perceived things in my life.

My perceptions, and my beliefs either caused me problems or liberated me. When I believed I was a victim I had problems, because I believed I had no choices.

I discovered that when I come from my authentic identity, problems disappear, because I can see that I always have choices. I can view any seeming difficulty as an opportunity for growth and development. I can see that in all things there is a gift.

I now know that I am more than flesh and blood. That I am the Presence of Life, Pure Love, Spirit, a Soul, a Child of God or the Universe, Divine Intelligence, or Mother Nature if you like. I am full of Infinite Possibility. That is what I am.

My real identity is that I am a powerful creator, Radical Self-Love, a Child of God!

In fact, I am the dynamic co-creator of my life! And what is true for me is equally and abundantly true for and about you!

Close your eyes for a minute. Focus your attention on your heart space and breath in and out. For just this second, entertain the possibility that you are the dynamic co-creator of your life.

What if at the core of your being you really and truly are Love and Goodness?

What if there really is a larger part of you that is deeply and completely present in this now moment and is intimately connected with everyone and everything?

What if you are magnificent and wonderful?

What if you really are powerfully creating your life right now?

What if?

It's true.

Saint Theresa of Avila once said, "Nothing can be compared to the great beauty and capabilities of a soul."

You are beautiful and capable beyond your wildest imaginings.

I invite you, just for a moment, to suspend any disbelief you have and join me in a short prayer. It doesn't matter at all if you "don't do" prayer. If that word bothers you, then just consider this an experiment in open-mindedness.

Think of it as a thought experiment.

Say this aloud with me now, "Please let me see the truth about me, no matter how magnificent it is."

You are magnificent! You are wonderful! You really are.

Are you willing to see yourself that way? If not, are you willing to be willing to see yourself that way?

You have nothing to lose except the disempowering lies you have been telling and believing about yourself.

You are magnificent and wonderful. It's OK if you don't know that. For now, know that I know it. You can learn to know it; actually, to remember it.

For simplicity sake, from here on out, I will refer to your true identity, what you really are, as your Radical Self-Love, Child of God Identity. I will refer to your origins, or "What you come from," as God/Spirit, unless I am quoting someone directly.

I realize the word God may carry a negative charge for you. It did for me. I will always use both terms when referring to either your identity or your origin.

If the word God really bothers you, use a sharpie to cross it out wherever it appears, or do the work I suggest to dissolve whatever story you have about that word.

It's just a word- really. I use it because it is convenient. Really. It doesn't matter what you call it.

Regardless of semantics, your authentic Self is Perfect, Whole, Complete, with nothing missing. When you were born, you arrived with everything necessary for your complete fulfillment and unique expression.

You are like an acorn which contains all the things it needs to become an oak tree. But unlike the acorn which has no choice but to transform, you must choose to grow the seeds within you. You must choose to grow into the magnificent oak tree that you are.

You must choose to come from your Radical Self-Love, Child of God Identity.

Who's doing it to you now?

> "You will know the truth, and the truth will set you free."
> – John 8:32

If you are still in love with the drop-of-sewage victim stories you are telling yourself, you may be like the character Smeagol in the Tolkien books The Hobbit and The Lord of the Rings.

Smeagol's prize possession was a ring he called "My Precious." His obsession with the ring transformed him from a kind and loving river Hobbit into a murderous and animalistic creature called Gollum. Gollum's insane relationship with "My Precious" caused him to live an isolated, miserable life, and lead to his untimely and violent death.

When coming from the victim identity, the drop-of-sewage victim stories are your own version of "My Precious"-the thing you cherish most; you think you can't live without. These drop-of-sewage victim stories about what happened, what "they" did or didn't do, what you yourself did or didn't do, become your obsession.

When you are in a victim mentality, you will hold onto, run away from, deny, defend or fight with these stories. You clutch onto them; you either wear them like a badge of honor, or desperately try to hide them from others or yourself. Either way, you mistakenly identify what has happened as who you are. It's not who you are.

You are not the drop-of-sewage victim stories you tell.

Say that out loud so you can hear yourself say it, **"I am not the drop-of-sewage stories I tell."** (It's OK if you aren't willing to believe this just yet. Keep reading anyway.)

You really aren't. Take a breath and let that sink in.

When you are in the victim identify you believe you are the victim sewage stories. Rather than working through hurts, forgiving yourself and/or others, you hold onto them. By holding on, you transform your victim sewage stories into "My Precious." When you do that you do yourself dirty.

I'm not condoning or approving of abuse, neglect, unkindness, injury, accident or illness. I am well aware that people sometimes experience horrific trauma. I'm not saying that these past events don't matter. They do. They are part of your experience. They can be the crucible in which you learn to come from your Radical Self-Love, Child of God Identity. Difficulty often facilitates the development of deep compassion.

Additionally, these experiences can be used to help others in similar circumstances. You can help them because you really understand where they are coming from, and if you have embraced your Radical Self-Love, Child of God Identity, you can show them how you did it.

But what of the things you see as "unforgivable?" What about those things that you are sure you can't forgive? What about when you believe others don't deserve to be forgiven because they are not remorseful? What about when you believe you yourself are unforgivable?

If you think about those things that you are unwilling to forgive, if you look straight at them, you may see a truth that was hiding in plain sight.

Who's doin it to you now?

The answer to this question is always the same: **"I am."**

By holding onto some past offense, you make yourself miserable in the present moment. You create and add the drop-of-sewage to your current life. OK let's be honest, sometimes it's more like a cup of sewage!

If you're anything like I was, you might react by clutching your "My Precious" drop of sewage story and self-pity all the tighter, in a perverse mea culpa kind of way. "I'm so bad and I can't help myself!"

NOT SO. It's simply not so.

But, as long as you are unwilling to challenge your victim beliefs, you will continue to create your life from them. No power for you. No freedom for you. No joy, peace, fulfillment, love, creativity for you- so sad.

You are a poor, poor pitiful victim. It's just that way.

You will never be able to complain your way into satisfaction, intimacy, and love.

Good luck with that.

In the movie version of The Hobbit, there is a scene in which the wizard Gandalf responds to the certainty that a badly behaving dwarf is "... under some dark spell!" He exhorts "You fool! He's under no enchantment but his own."

Ponder that for a moment... Take a deep breath.

You are under no enchantment but your own!

EXCUSE ME, BUT HOW MUCH DOES THAT VICTIM IDENTITY COST?

> "No one in your life is stopping you from fulfilling your dream of becoming a lion tamer."
> – David Casteal

For me, the cost of coming from the victim identity was exceedingly high. The victim identity was so pervasive it was pretty much everywhere in my life. The saying "How you do anything is how you do everything," certainly applied to me.

I had no say; or rather I believed I had no say about how my life went. I looked to others to make decisions for me, or at least approve of the decisions I made.

I was sad, depressed, resigned and full of self-pity. I was physically exhausted and emotionally unstable. I felt off-balance and ill at ease most of the time. I didn't love or even like myself much. I engaged in self-destructive isolating behaviors like compulsive eating, shopping, and movie watching.

My love relationships were serially monogamous, but in general, they all had intense highs followed by heart wrenching lows- an endless cycle. There was little true intimacy. I wouldn't allow myself to be seen and known. I was not receptive to real love and connection. In one particularly dramatic relationship there were nine break-ups. Good God, no wonder I was exhausted!

I spent little or no time pursuing creativity, recreation, or art. I ran myself into debt. I had no peace of mind or sense of purpose. I engaged in little or no spiritual development or self-reflection. I experienced only fleeting moments of happiness, joy and freedom.

I knew I loved people, intellectually, but I couldn't really feel it. I just couldn't stand being me one more minute. That's when I said the "Please God help me, I can't live like this!" prayer, and God/Spirit, stepped in with "Stop being stupid!"

What's it costing you?

I invite you to get buck-naked honest with yourself about what coming from the victim identity is costing you. I can almost guarantee that until you see the cost clearly, and really get the impact it has on your life, you will not be willing to do the necessary inner work to "Stop Being Stupid."

"What's one drop of sewage, right?

"After all," you may think, "Isn't it OK to indulge in coming from a victim identity some of the time? I kind of enjoy complaining," you might protest. "You just don't understand. My complaints are legitimate."

Of course you can choose as you wish, but you want to get very clear about what you are choosing when you cling to the myth that you have no choice.

I invite you to get some paper and a pen and do some writing about what the victim identity is costing you right now. I did not say think about it, or type it into your laptop or tablet, I said write it down on a piece of paper.

Writing involves your body, mind and emotions in ways that just thinking or typing does not. There is something very personal about physically writing. There is nothing to distance you from what you are expressing. Physically writing about these things can help you to be truly honest. Besides, scientific research shows that simply writing about your feelings is beneficial. So doing this exercise can only help you.

Write about what life is like in the areas of: relationships, love, creativity, freedom, peace of mind, spirituality, personal and professional satisfaction and fulfillment, and health.

Here are some questions that can assist you in seeing the cost of coming from the victim identity in these important areas of life. Write the answers down and read them back to yourself.

- What do I experience in my relationships with lovers, spouses, children, other family members, friends, co-workers, bosses, customers, etc.? How would I like these relationships to be different?
- Do I have dreams or a life purpose? How have I pursued this purpose? What are these dreams? What motivates my daily life?
- If I have no dreams, purpose, or motivation what is it like to live a life without those things?
- What is my level of physical wellbeing? Am I physically healthy? Do I eat well and exercise regularly? Do I get enough rest and relaxation? How well do I sleep at night? Do I love my body? Do I know how to play? Do I play? Explain. What is this area of my life like for me?
- Am I financially responsible? Do I have enough to meet my obligations and to share with others? Have I been responsible for insuring my future financial wellbeing? What is this area of life like for me?
- What is my relationship like with myself? Do I like and love myself? What is that like for me? Do I have any kind of religious or spiritual practice? Do I experience peace of mind? What is it like for me?

Remember the point here is to see what the victim identity is costing you, not to beat yourself up. It may not *"feel"* good to look honestly at the costs of the victim identity, but it is a necessary part of the process.

If you have never done this kind of self-reflection, I would suggest you do this writing in several sittings. You may want to work on one set of questions at a time, and discuss what you have learned with a trusted friend or advisor. If you don't have someone like that, no worries, it isn't necessary.

I did not have a trusted spiritual advisor or mentor until I met Charles. By the way, it took me another couple weeks to ask him to help me. I had therapists and doctors, but I lied to them because I didn't want them to think badly of me. As you continue this process, you will develop those kinds of relationships if you want them. Here's why you will attract them, because having those kinds of relationships will be consistent with your new beliefs.

I promise you that the discomfort of this kind of work turns into relief as you continue the transformational process. Remember every caterpillar dissolves in the cocoon before it transforms into a butterfly. From the caterpillar's point of view, that process must seem devastating and horrible, but it is necessary. So, whether you did or didn't do the writing, it's OK my sweet caterpillar. I invite you to be gentle with yourself.

Right now I would like you to literally wrap your arms around yourself. Take a deep breath, hold it for a beat and then slowly exhale. Now close your eyes and give yourself a long hug and say, "I love you. Thank you for being so brave and honest." Take another deep breath and hold it for a beat and then slowly exhale. (It's OK if you don't mean it yet. Just try it anyways!)

If that was uncomfortable, or you just couldn't do it, that's OK too. No worries. Your journey has begun.

This is a great beginning!

I love you and I stand for your greatness. Even if all you do is continue to read, or even if you throw the book in the creek, it is a perfect beginning! Thank you for being so brave and honest!

What's the pay off?

If you have been honest with yourself even a little, you are probably becoming keenly aware that the victim identity costs you a lot. But even if you truly desire something new, you will likely balk.

You may be thinking, "Wow, why would I do that? Coming from the victim identity is crazy! I ought to stop." You're right, it is crazy, and it is costing you your life. Clearly you would not do it if you weren't getting something out of it.

Apparently you are getting something out of it.

You may disagree. I imagine you may say something like "No, no your wrong! I'm miserable! I'm not getting anything out of this! You're the crazy one!"

Think again.

When I looked at my life, I saw that I chose the victim identity for three major reasons:

1)   I got to be right about everything.

2) It was very familiar and thus felt comfortably safe.

3) It was the perfect excuse for avoiding any responsibility for my life.

Playing a victim meant I never had to show up for anything or anyone, not really. I avoided being vulnerable like the plague. I didn't want to get hurt. I was all about safety. I would often make pre-emptive strikes. I would end relationships to avoid the possibility of being *"rejected,"* and then tell a victim sewage story that seemed to legitimize blaming them.

I invite you to take a minute and write about those three possible benefits of coming from the victim identity. The following questions may be helpful.

- What, or who am I vehemently right about? Am I being right about a particular person (myself included), situation, issue, idea or institution?
- Am I habitually miserable? Is it familiar for me to feel sad, angry, self-pitying or depressed?
- Do I use the victim identity to avoid being honest or vulnerable? Do I blame others for my dishonesty?
- Do I have a sense of real purpose? Do I prefer to follow other people's instructions about what I should be doing with my life so I can blame them when it doesn't *"work out"*?
- What are the *"good"* reasons I have for why I can't pursue my dreams?

Read your answers back to yourself out loud. Let it sink in. Again I invite you to share with a trusted friend or advisor. The purpose of this writing is to see exactly how you get in your own way blocking your authentic self-expression. It is not about beating yourself up. Beating yourself up is victim identity behavior.

Again, I thank you for being willing to look for yourself. I thank you for being honest with yourself. I thank you for reading this far.

In my experience seeing what I got out of playing the victim was powerful. It gave me access to taking full responsibility. It allowed me to see and to remember that I had a choice.

It's not in the least bit fun or flattering to look honestly at yourself when you've had a habit of looking the other way. I can only tell you that what seemed to be the worst day of my life, ended up being a portal for transformation-a caterpillar to butterfly beginning.

I wish I could tell you that my life changed on a dime in that instant, but that would be a lie. The transformation has been slow; as I've said, I've done it long and messy. I did not have a guide that had made all the mistakes that I have made and could help me avoid them.

You do. I'm that kind of guide.

I'm the one who can tell you what doesn't work, and what does work because I've done both.

My intention for you is that you might learn from my mistakes, so that you can transform with velocity if you choose. It takes work, and I can teach you how to do it if you are willing.

You've gotten a taste of the work. Not fun, but necessary.

You're worth the work!

CHAPTER 2 SUMMARY

- The victim identity is disempowering and no fun for those around you.
- The victim identity produces life experiences that are safe, predictable but ultimately dissatisfying.
- Your life experiences are the result of your beliefs.
- You are not the victim identity.
- You are not your experiences, thoughts, mind, body, emotions, and feelings.
- You can experience your true identity by being still and focusing on your breath in this now moment.
- Your repetitive thoughts become beliefs.
- Your beliefs dictate your way of being.
- Your way of being dictates your actions.
- Your actions produce your life experiences.
- You see what you believe.
- You are a powerful creator of your life experiences.
- You are the common denominator to all of the problems in your life.
- Your authentic identity is *Radical Self-Love, a Child of God*.
- Your origin, or "What you come from", is God/Spirits.

- Holding onto the drop-of-sewage stories keeps you in the victim identity.
- Choosing the victim identity has steep costs.
- The victim identity robs you of intimacy, love, creativity, freedom, peace of mind, spirituality, personal and professional satisfaction and fulfillment, and optimal health.
- Most often you choose the victim identity in order to: be right about something; feel safe or comfortable; or avoid taking responsibility for your life.

Chapter 3
Pre-Requisites for Transformation

Are you ready to drop the Blame Game?

> *"If I knew better, then I'd do better."*
> – Anonymous

Blaming and complaining are the quintessential behaviors of someone who is coming from a victim identity. They are the most prevalent forms of sewage that get added to your life.

So the million-dollar question is- Are you willing? Or are you at least willing to be willing to stop blaming and complaining?

Note, I did not suggest that you in fact know how to stop doing this, nor that you recognize it as inauthentic. Those behaviors are inauthentic because they are un-loving. They are inconsistent with your *Radical Self-Love, Child of God Identity*.

How many times have I heard, or said, *"She/he should've known better"*? Well, apparently they didn't-obviously! And therein lies my path to freedom. If I stand on the premise that if I knew better I'd do better, then it must be true of others, ALL others. I don't mean knowing about something intellectually, I mean in your heart. It's like the difference between knowing about ice cream, and actually having tasted it.

When I am unwilling to cut others slack, to forgive, it's because I am unwilling to forgive myself. For some reason, I think I should be perfect, or never make a mistake. I beat myself up and you're not far behind.

I just didn't know any better, until I did.

You see, I am perfect, and so are you. Everyone is perfect.

No. That was not a misprint.

I said everyone is perfect.

I make perfect mistakes. I say the perfectly wrong thing. I feel perfectly miserable at times. Perfect does not mean good or bad.

Perfect means accurate, without flaw.

So give it up. You're already perfect. You are exactly, perfectly the way you are, and you are exactly, perfectly not the way you are not.

Again, perfect simply means accurate, without flaw. You are, without any flaw, exactly, accurately the way you are right now. At this moment you may be exactly, accurately angry and frustrated. And if you are angry and frustrated, you are flawlessly angry and frustrated.

In other words, things that are going on in life; people, places and things are just the way they are and just the way they are not.

That includes you.

Complaining and blaming puts you at odds with the way things are. It is an attempt to fight reality. It is to say in essence *"Things shouldn't be the way they are!"*

Fair enough, but they are.

How insane is it to fight what is? You can never, ever win that fight. Transformation is entirely possible, but first you must accept what is.

Acceptance of what is brings peace.

Taking complete responsibility for your life provides access to acceptance and taking powerful action if necessary. Accepting things exactly as they are, and exactly as they are not is the pre-requisite to any meaningful transformation.

You cannot transform something you are running from, denying, hating or fighting.

My question to you is-Are you willing to take responsibility for the consequences of your, at times, *"perfectly"* destructive behaviors?

Or, do you want to keep blaming and complaining? Do you choose the victim identity with its blaming and complaining sewage stories, or *your Radical Self-Love, Child of God Identity?*

I want you to try something for ten minutes. For ten whole minutes refrain from any blaming and complaining out loud or in your head. If that seems too difficult try it for just five minutes.

Set your timer. I mean it. Really, just try it for five minutes.

What was that like for you? Wouldn't you like to be free of that endlessly, futile battle?

If I knew better, I'd do better. If they knew better they'd do better.

This premise, can gently help you lighten up, and not take everything so personally, even your own *"mistakes."*

Again, it's a matter of willingness. Are you willing, or willing to be willing to give up your right to judge, blame and punish yourself and others? Are you willing to stop blaming and complaining?

"But, but, but..." You might say, *"You don't understand! That guy really is an asshole! He really hurt me! My parents, boyfriend, girlfriend, wife, husband, kids, in-laws, boss, really are doing it to me! They are to blame and I'm right about it!"*

Fantastic! You're right-you win. (Notice how automatically that being right thing comes up. Hello!)

But really, you lose. You lose power, love, peace, affection, connection, and freedom- in short, your life.

Do you want to be right or happy?

I said this to my niece one time and she tearfully said, *"Being right is being happy!"*

I beg to differ. There may be a certain satisfaction in playing the judge, jury and executioner with the people in your life, including yourself, but it will never make you feel happy, loving or deeply connected to others. This short-lived pleasure kills off relationships with blame and complaint.

Do you want to be right or happy? Do you want sewage or *Radical Self-Love?* Do you want the victim identity, or *Radical Self-Love, Child of God Identity?*

How do I transform?

"Be transformed by the renewal of your mind."
– Romans 12:2

"Let it be done for you according to your faith."
– Matthew 9:29

The short and the long of it is HABIT.

So what's a habit?

A **habit** *is a constant often unconscious inclination to perform an act acquired through its frequent repetition.*

Habit: your best friend, or your worst enemy depending on the nature of the habits you've created.

The down side of any habit is that it blinds you to what is really present in any given moment.

Check it out. When you walk into your home, you don't really see what's there. You see what you expect to see, what you habitually see. You automatically see the patterns of the things you *"know"* are usually there.

You don't walk in and say to yourself, chair, chair, chair, blue cushion, brown coach, table, glass, floor, ceiling, curtain, window, glass pane, dog, cat. No, you take it in all at once without a thought; your brain fills in the details-habitually. You see your living room the way you always see it. You see what you believe, you do not believe what you see.

I'll say that again, because it is counter-intuitive.

You see things the way you believe they are, not the way they actually are.

For example, my house was broken into about three years ago. I came home from work as usual, just doing my thing. I didn't see that several prominent knick-knacks were missing in my sitting room for over three hours. I walked in and out of there four or five times before I noticed. I saw what I believed would be there, not what was actually there. My brain filled in the images of the missing objects.

Prove it to yourself right now. This is a passage from the website www.livescience.com.

S1M1L4RLY, YOUR M1ND 15 R34D1NG 7H15
4U70M471C4LLY W17H0U7 3V3N 7H1NK1NG 4B0U7 17.

Your brain had little or no trouble dealing with that passage because of the way it processes information. It has you see what you expect to see. It uses previously known patterns to analyze and interpret everything.

We do the same thing with people, situations and things. We see what we believe them to be, what we have already decided about them. We use our very own personal automatic pilot: our habits.

When we run on habit we often miss what is actually there. We look at our spouse or friend or boss and we already *"know"* what they are like, how they *"are."* My wife is a nag, my boss is demanding, my children are lazy and so on. So even if they behave differently, we don't see it. We see them the way we always do, and so we experience them the way we expect to, not the way they really are.

For example I knew my dad was *"a control freak!"* So no matter what he said to me I believed that he was always telling me what to do, and judging me. He would ask me questions about my life, how I was doing, etc. and I would react like it was the Spanish Inquisition. I would get defensive and angry and tell him to mind his own business or leave me alone. I complained about him and blamed him for our relationship being "rocky."

Once I saw that habit of belief ("He's *a control freak!*") and understood what it was costing me, I did the work to drop it and create a new habit of belief about him: "He's *always loving and supportive!*" Get it. I created a new belief that gave me a new experience, one that I wanted.

Once that belief got activated, became a habit, I started seeing his questions as an expression of his love and concern for me. I began to have an altogether different experience of that relationship.

My dad recently died. I had the privilege of being with him when he passed. It was beautiful. He was at home surrounded by his loving family, at peace and was no longer in pain.

I miss my dad. Our relationship has been good, really good for years. There was nothing left unsaid. I have absolutely no regrets regarding my dad. I believe that he is closer to me now than he was in life. I talk to him all the time and I believe he is still watching over me.

It doesn't matter if these beliefs are *"true."* What's important is that they empowered me to have a joyous experience of my dad even through his illness and death. I love you Popee!

Imagine how that might have been for my dad and me if I had continued to see him as just "a *control freak.*"

Who in your life have you consigned to the scrap heap as just a label? What parts of yourself have you likewise judged and labeled?

Take a minute and think about that-write down their names and the labels you've assigned them. I'll wait.

Is it possible that you are wrong about some of these people or yourself? If you keep it up, you will never really see or know them. You will never really see or know yourself either. It is part of what the victim identity is costing you.

Give yourself a moment to think about that. Take a breath.

You can begin again. Right now in this moment, you can start over. Any relationship can be made new if you choose. (I will teach you how to do that kind of work. You're doing really well. It takes real courage to look at yourself honestly!)

Most actions have their origins in what you are thinking and believing about your self, and your life- habitually.

If you think a thought, repeatedly, with enough emotion, it becomes a habitual way of thinking, which then solidifies into a belief.

Habitual beliefs become your personal laws. Your personal laws determine how you operate in life; they determine how you perceive and react to everything.

If, through frequent repetition you have developed the habit of thinking and believing you are a victim, then your habitual actions will reflect that habitual belief. It becomes a self-fulfilling prophecy.

Everything in your life will perfectly reflect your beliefs: your behaviors, perceptions, points of view, opinions, emotional experiences, relationships, physical health, etc.

It is done unto you AS you believe.

When this concept finally sunk in, I remember feeling sick to my stomach and thinking: I am so screwed! I had created this miserable mess of a life, and I knew that I would continue to do so because of my habits.

Again, this is normal. It is why most human beings create the same dreary patterns in life: the same bad relationship with different people; the same demanding and incompetent bosses with different jobs; the same ten or twenty pounds lost and gained over and over again.

There is nothing you can do to get rid of a habit, once it's established. After all, a habit is an unconscious behavior; you don't even realize you are doing it. It has become automatic.

Your nervous system has created pathways that reflect these habits of thought. Your repetitive thoughts, feelings and behaviors have hard wired your brain and body to produce these patterns automatically. In other words, your brain and body are in on this deal.

Thankfully there is a way out. An undesirable habit can be replaced with a different habit, a habit that produces the results you want, not the results you don't want. That is precisely what I did with my dad. Creating a new habit means practicing new thoughts, behaviors and emotions until they become automatic.

It is an axiom of neuro-science that neurons that fire together wire together. Thus wiring the neurons in a new habit pattern requires firing those new patterns repeatedly. Additionally, when you stop firing the old patterns, like anything else those connections atrophy.

In other words, you have to practice a new thought until it becomes a habit. Over time, your brain and body will *"memorize"* whatever you practice consistently and *"forget"* the things that you don't practice.

The body can be a great ally. There is an old saying, *Bring the body and the mind will follow.* As you just read, science is now proving this. If you practice new behavior, even if your thoughts are still coming from the constellation of victim beliefs, the body will teach the brain and emotions to *"get in line"* so to speak.

Hence the idea, *"Fake it, till you make it,"* carries new promise and significance.

I am not talking about being inauthentic. I am talking about behaving in ways that are consistent with your authentic *Radical Self-Love, Child of God identity.* It is critical to do this even when it's uncomfortable. If your behavior is *Radically Self-Loving,* even when you don't *"feel"* like it, you can train your brain, and body to come from your authentic *Radical Self-Love, Child of God identity,* habitually.

The question may arise, *"What happens to the old habits?"* Think of it this way, it is as if you've put them on a back shelf. The pathways are there, but when you stop using them they cease to be highly functional. You can, however re-activate them through practice. That is why continued deep practice of desirable habits is necessary.

The more you practice thinking thoughts consistent with your authentic identity, the easier it becomes to think those type of thoughts.

The less you practice thinking thoughts consistent with the victim identity, the harder it becomes to think those type of thoughts.

This is terrific news!

But, since choice is a function of consciousness, if you are unaware of your beliefs, then you have no choice.

As Reverend Michael Bernard Beckwith has said, *"It's not what you don't know that hurts you, it's what you know that just ain't so."*

You do have a say, but not if you believe you don't, or are oblivious.

"Wait" you might say, *"I think I'm oblivious most of the time! Thanks a lot! So if I don't know what's running me, how am I supposed to stop being stupid? How am I supposed to stop adding the drop of sewage victim thoughts, beliefs and actions to my glass of life? How am I to develop these new habits?"*

In general, when you play the victim-identity card, you are running with an underlying belief that is inherently false. The reason it kicks your ass and feels so awful, is that it is fundamentally in opposition to your true *Radical Self-Love, Child of God Identity.*

Rolling with a victim identity feels off, inauthentic, out of whack, constricting and otherwise dreadful. Recognition of the victim-identity habitual beliefs, thoughts, stories, and behaviors is critical but often elusive.

It's as if you are slipping yourself a "sewage" mickey.

It takes effort to recognize what is really there in your life rather than seeing things habitually through the lens of your victim identity and it's stories. You have to look again.

You deserve to take a second look, to make a better choice.

But how do you do that?

How indeed?

Chapter 3 Summary

- Blaming and Complaining are hallmarks of the victim identity.
- Knowing about something is not the same as knowing it in your heart.
- When you know better, you do better.
- You are perfect.
- Blaming and complaining is an attempt to fight reality.
- Fighting reality is insane. You can never win that fight.
- You must be willing to give up your right to blame and complain in order to come from your *Radical Self-Love, Child of God Identity.*
- Habits are unconscious inclinations to perform a particular action- they are automatic.
- Habits can be empowering or disempowering depending on the nature of the habit.
- Habits can blind you to reality and limit what's possible in your experience.
- *Your habit of blaming and complaining* has steep costs in your relationships.
- Habits of thoughts become beliefs. You take actions and view life based on your beliefs, which is how you create your life.
- Your brain and body become habituated to your beliefs.
- The only way to get rid of a disempowering habit is to replace it with an empowering habit.
- The body can help teach the brain a new habit.
- Deep practice is necessary to acquire a new habit.
- Choice is a function of awareness or consciousness.

Chapter 4
How do I know when I'm adding a Drop of Sewage?

Being aware of Patterns

Victim-identity behavior patterns are the result of failing to accept life the way it is, and/or failing to take responsibility for your behavior.

You are either unwilling to accept what is happening (along with you're feelings about it); or you are unwilling to take a doable action. These are the two ways you attempt to avoid responsibility for your life.

When you step into the victim shoes, and lace them up you do one of the following: you fight, deny, hate or run from your experience.

So how do you *"Stop Being Stupid"* in these particular ways?

For starters, you've got to know you have a problem.

Awareness is the key to freedom. If you can recognize your victim identity patterns, then you're less likely to buy your stories of woe and intrigue as *"THE TRUTH."*

There are many behavior patterns that act as *"red flags."* They can warn you that you are either engaging in the victim identity or about to do so.

The victim identity, sewage patterns I engaged in centered around taking care of others, particularly men and refusing to take care of myself, or ignoring my own life, and my own business. I also engaged in a variety of self-destructive behaviors.

Everyone else came first. I was at the bottom of my *"to do"* list. My business was simply not a priority.

I will list and describe for you some of my victim-identity patterns. They are the *"red flags"* that let me know when I am coming from a victim identity, adding a drop of sewage to my life.

Recognizing the *"red flags"* gives me access to taking responsibility for my experience, without which I have no choice but to play the victim.

When I engage in these patterns of thought, belief and behavior, it is impossible to come from my authentic *Radical Self-Love, Child of God Identity.*

The purpose of this section is to help you identify your *"red flags."* I'm clear about mine. I write about them here in detail with the hope that it will help you to see something for yourself about yourself.

There may be additional behaviors you may engage in that also come from the victim identity. In general, any behaviors that involve the following also stem from the victim identity: blaming; complaining; judging; feeling guilty or shameful; and any behaviors that have you experience a loss of power or freedom.

You may engage in only one, a few, or many of the patterns described. You may think, *"Hey, I'm not so bad, I only engage in the victim identity a little."* OK, but remember, it only takes a tiny drop of sewage to taint your glass of life.

I suggest you read this section with the following questions in mind and then write down your answers as you go so you can see them in black and white:

- Do I behave like that or have I acted like that in the past? Explain.
- Do I see similar patterns of thought or behavior in my life? Explain.

THE USUAL SUSPECTS AND THEIR ALIAS' (AKA) (ALSO KNOWN AS)

People Pleasing: (AKA: The Chameleon/Narcissist)
Manipulation and Control: (AKA: The Control Freak!)
Caretaking/Rescuing: (AKA: The Super Hero)
Hyper-responsibility: (AKA: It's my fault!)
Poll-taking (AKA: Waffling and Indecisiveness)
Busyness: (AKA: The Squirrel)
Complaining and Judging: (AKA: The Perfectionist)
Self-Neglect and or Destructive Behaviors: (AKA: The Martyr)
Hypersensitivity: (AKA: The Drama Queen or King)
Combativeness: (AKA: The Rebel)
Wishful Thinking: (AKA: The Pessimist)
Resignation and Detachment: (AKA: The Fatalist)

People Pleasing: (AKA: The Chameleon/Narcissist)

"A bucket that is turned upside down, even in a cloud-burst will not be filled."
– Ernest Holmes

"To love and be loved is to feel the sun from both sides."
– David Viscott

I was, and can be, a master at reading a crowd. I would adapt myself to fit in. I would tell them what they wanted to hear, use the language or lingo necessary to mimic and thus fit in with any person or group. In other words, I was a fake. I would do what it took to please, gain acknowledgment, praise, or validation from those around me.

I wanted your attention. I defined myself, my value and worth, by the kind and amount of attention I got. I would use your response, or what I thought you thought of me, to either validate or invalidate my opinions, goals, choices and behaviors. *"Look at me, look at me! Please, someone see me! Love me!"* is what I was really trying to communicate.

When coming from the victim identity I was seldom if ever authentically expressing myself, my me-ness. I would edit myself, hiding parts I thought might not be acceptable and pretending to have the qualities I thought were prized by you or your group.

Thus, even if you did love me, I couldn't accept it. I didn't believe you. I was sure that if you really knew me, you wouldn't love me. So I stayed hidden; I never let you see or know me. I was sad and lonely- even in a crowd.

It's much nicer to live with my bucket turned right side up, and to both give and receive love. I get to feel that warmth inside and out.

Manipulation and Control: (AKA: The Control Freak!)

If I didn't get the response I thought I wanted, I would express anger or disapproval or disappointment. I would attempt to get you to do what I wanted, or stop doing what I didn't like.

I'd say things like *"you hurt my feelings,"* or I'd withdraw. At other times I'd become uncommunicative, or accuse you of manipulating me. Or I'd tell myself you were abandoning me or rejecting me or disrespecting or neglecting me. I'd think I was being treated badly and wallow in dramatic self-pity. I might engage in silent scorn or slam doors, leaving without a word, or cry.

I might offer unsolicited advice, and then be offended when you weren't appropriately grateful, or didn't do what I suggested. I sometimes would make plans for you, taking actions that weren't mine to take, always for your own good, don't you know. I would even answer questions for you as if you couldn't speak for yourself, or do things for you without being asked. I just knew what was best, and I was sure you would be ever so grateful.

If you protested, disagreed or failed to show *"appropriate gratitude"* I'd get angry and hurt all over again, and again, and again.

I consistently attempted to orchestrate people and situations in ways that would make me *"feel"* important, wanted, needed, and loved. I was rarely authentically creative, loving or truly collaborative.

In the end, there was never enough of what I thought I needed for me to feel whole.

Caretaking/Rescuing: (AKA: The Super Hero)

"What's the difference between a co-dependent and a pit-bull?
Eventually the pit-bull will let go."
– Anonymous

The manipulation and controlling behaviors dovetailed nicely into engaging in caretaking and rescuing. I would treat you, especially if you were a man I was dating or married to, like you were incapable of taking care of yourself.

I'm not talking about helping people in an empowering way. I'm not talking about being kind and generous with no strings attached. I'm not talking about being of service to others, as in helping people help themselves. I'm talking about behaviors that enable others to be irresponsible and/or insincere.

I would regularly do for you, what any grown person is expected to do for themselves. I would *"help"* when you didn't ask, (I could just tell you needed it.) I would plan and do things I was sure you needed done. I would do things like buying your groceries, or cleaning your house, or doing your laundry, or cooking your meals, or getting an application and filling it out for you, or buying you anything from sports equipment to a car. I was just helping you get started. I was just monitoring to make sure you were on track.

I used your inaction as a source of judgment, which allowed me a certain feeling of comfortable superiority. I would engage in conversations with you or in my head saying things like *"Look what I've done for you! And see how ungrateful you are! It's such a one-way street. You never appreciate the things I do."*

I would act like a bean counter of conditional love. Bartering and scamming and wallowing in a sticky morass of self-pity, righteously miserable about how generous I was, and how you'd *"done me wrong"* one more time. I was firmly entrenched in my victim kingdom, the realm of ever expanding DOOM. Sheesh! What a drag! No real love was possible.

What I was really after was being needed. I wanted you to depend on me, to need me. Deep down I was sure that if you didn't need me, you wouldn't want or love me. I believed I had to earn your love. I wanted you to see how important I was to you.

I wanted you to get that.

What I failed to see, to get, was that the more I neglected my life the less important I felt to myself. I remember talking to a friend of mine and in tearful frustration describing myself as a mere accessory to other people's lives.

Hyper-responsibility (AKA: It's my fault!)

I used to think that if you were my friend, family member, significant other, co-worker, student, coach, or barista it was my job to make sure you were happy and pleased with me. Your happiness and your opinion of me was not only my business- it was my responsibility!

Thus, when there was a *"problem"* it was always my fault, and I do mean always. I had that kind of power, so I thought.

I remember shortly after I began working with my spiritual director Reverend Maggie, I was whining to her about the man I was dating, and she broke in and said *"Yes, yes, yes, Carol, it is all your fault! In fact, the Peloponnesian War was your fault too."*

It was another *"Stop Being Stupid"* moment. I began to laugh, because I could see how ridiculous I was being. In my mind, if I was just good enough or pretty enough or had bigger boobs, or I hadn't said this, or I had said that, or worked out harder, or bought a burrito instead of enchiladas, then people would treat me right and value me.

It was everywhere in my life. At work, I would take the heaviest teaching loads and work longer and harder than anyone I knew. I went above and beyond my duties. YOU should take care of yourself in terms of having weekends and evenings off, and staying home if you're sick, but not me.

I had a multitude of friendships in which I was providing most of the effort. I believed it was all on me. I would make the phone calls, drive the further distance to meet, make the plans, adapt my schedule, and feel guilty if I said no, to anyone, for any reason.

You could always count on me. Always available to help move, or visit or drive the car, or drop off at the airport, or house sit or take care of the dog or cat. I was willing to give, a lot, but disinclined to receive anyone's help. I felt guilty if I asked for or accepted help. I thought I should be able to handle everything, and anything myself.

All I wanted in return was to be treated the way I wanted, and it never quite worked out for me. And of course that was my fault too. I just wasn't enough... or so I believed.

Poll-taking (AKA: Waffling and Indecisiveness)

Poll taking is a corollary to the people-pleasing theorem. I believed I had to have people's approval to make decisions. I didn't know I could choose.

When faced with a decision, I believed that I had to have enough people agreeing with the decision, or a good enough reason to justify it.

I would go from person to person to person. What do you think I should do? What about you? And you? God forbid there be disagreement, then I'd have to talk to a lot more people to get a super majority!

I felt the need to justify and defend any decision I made. I had a near inability to give a simple no to any request, believing I must have a convincing enough reason. That went for things as simple as declining a coffee date to putting a $30,000 cash advance on my credit cards, for a *"business"* loan for a *"good friend."* Ouch! One of my mentors told me, *"That so called loan, was cheap tuition."*

I wish I could say that I got the *"lesson"* I paid for with that experience, but unfortunately that was not the last time I gave away money I couldn't afford to loan. As I've said, my journey has been long. I've been stupid a lot!

I am happy to say I no longer *"loan"* money. I know how to be generous after I've paid my expenses, from the over-flow.

There is an old saying, *"If you stand for nothing, you'll fall for anything."* That is especially true if you play the victim and won't take a stand for yourself.

Busyness: (AKA: The Squirrel)

> *"There is more to life than just speeding it up."*
> – Gandhi

As you can imagine, with those kinds of behavior patterns, I was extraordinarily busy. I'm not knocking productivity or being a hard worker. It's awesome to accomplish things, live full out, and contribute! The kind of busyness

I refer to is something altogether different. It was frenetic, driven behaviors born out of a belief that I had to *"do"* my way into worthiness.

Additionally, this busyness served another very important purpose in the victim identity; it afforded little or no time for silence, stillness or self-reflection. No time to simply be with myself.

My life was structured in such a task oriented, crisis management way that I rarely got present to how little satisfaction, fulfillment, peace and joy I had in my life. In fact, I could barely stand to be alone with my thoughts. If I was alone, I always had to have the TV or radio, or music on. Anytime I got the faintest whiff of my dissatisfaction, my inner dis-ease, I'd take on yet another project with its requisite flurry of activity. I was making myself miserable.

I just didn't see it.

I was firmly entrenched in the NCAA (No Clue At All).

Complaining, Judging and Blaming: (AKA: The Perfectionist)

"If you judge people you will never have time to learn to love them."
– Mother Theresa

"If you focus on the faults of others, you are the one who suffers for them."
– Eugene Weisner

True that.

All of these people, places, busyness, etc. led me to the inescapable conclusion that, as a friend of mine used to say, *"Life's a bitch, and then you are one."* There was just an awful lot about life, my life in particular, that I didn't like or approve of. In addition to complaining about, judging and blaming myself, I disapproved of others too.

Life just wasn't going my way. I let anyone who would listen hear the latest installment about how, *"They were doing it to me again."* And how they *"Don't do things right!"*

Additionally, I was deathly afraid of making mistakes. The way I saw it, you'd better do things right or don't do them at all. And do it right the first time! And for heaven sakes don't ask any questions, you might look stupid.

I had a cadre of people in my life with whom I gossiped, judged and complained about: my significant other, my family, my other friends, myself, work, the government, the weather, traffic, the Republicans, rich people, the Police, current events, traffic, etc., nothing was off limits.

Complaining is not the same as productive *"venting,"* which can be a powerful tool for working through an upset. (I will discuss venting in Chapter 9.)

In short, I had created a culture of complaint around me. We would take turns complaining, judging, blaming, analyzing and being *"right."* We were *"right"* about ourselves, (victims) and others (perpetrators). We were *"right"* about what needed to change about others, and how we ourselves needn't. We defended and explained away our inappropriate behaviors as justifiable reactions to others. After all, they were to blame.

At times, this behavior left me feeling comfortably superior, self-satisfied and fond of the person I was gossiping with. At other times it left me feeling defensive, and angry, or despairing, sad, guilty and shameful. At all times, no matter how juicy the gossip, or how deserving the judgment and blame, I was ultimately left with a sense of resignation and varying degrees of depression.

The seductive beliefs that fueled this cycle were:

If someone or something out there would act right, or *"be"* different, I would be free to be "*me*", and then I'd be happy.

If I just talked about it enough, then I'd figure out how to make them change.

Self-Neglect and Destructive Behaviors: (AKA: The Martyr)

As all of this was going on, as I was minding everyone else's business, no one was minding the shop. Lights were on, but no one was home in my life.

I did not tend to the well being of my body. My nutrition was inconsistent, and I never got enough rest. My bills were often paid late, not because I didn't have the money, but because I'd lose track of things. My physical surroundings, my apartment, car, and desk, were often messy. I had run myself into debt attempting to buy other people's affection with gifts or by taking on their financial obligations.

When I felt sadness, guilt, shame or anger I would often engage in self-indulgent, and/or self-destructive behavior. I'd binge eat, and was bulimic in my early twenties. Occasionally, I would spend money recklessly or buy extravagant gifts for myself. I would get involved with men I wasn't interested in, or have sex when I didn't want to, or have sex in ways I didn't want to.

I would call people names. I thought it was perfectly legitimate to *"Tell people about themselves."* I had to learn that I was merely stating my opinion. This kind of retaliation would temporarily give me a feeling of satisfaction, but I was ultimately left feeling more empty and off-balance than I had felt before *"I let them have it."*

I was ruthless and relentless with the coulda, shoulda, woulda, conversations with myself. I would compulsively re-think past conversations, coming up with all of the snappy or poignant things I could have or should have said, but didn't.

Sometimes I would fantasize elaborate conversations or scenarios that I thought ought to take place- pure wishful thinking. I'd think of all the things I could have done, or should have said. I was sure things would be better if I could come up with the *"right"* combination and do that.

I would call myself names out loud and in my head- especially if I made any mistakes. I would tell myself that I wasn't good enough, pretty enough, that I was stupid and worthless.

I held grudges against myself.

There were innumerable things I had done, or thought I had done about which I felt guilt, shame and remorse.

I couldn't run fast enough from what I thought I'd done, and who I thought I was. That's when I got desperate enough to say that little prayer- *"Dear God help me, I can't live like this."*

Hypersensitivity: (AKA: The Drama Queen or King)

I was often convinced that your actions were all about me.

EVERYTHING WAS PERSONAL.

I personalized the normal life pains of loss, or failing to achieve a particular goal.

It was MY PAIN rather than the pain of growing up.

I didn't just fail, I WAS a FAILURE.

People didn't die or leave, they ABANDONED me, or REJECTED me.

You didn't have a right to your opinion of me if I didn't agree with it, you DISRESPECTED me or you HURT ME or my feelings.

I didn't have an opinion about your behavior, you MADE ME ANGRY! Or you're an ASSHOLE!

I am not closed-minded; you just don't know what you're talking about. I'm RIGHT!

I absolutely believed that whatever I was feeling, and the story I was telling myself about it, was true. It was the TRUTH.

Me, me, me! I'm wasn't opinionated and self-centered, I'm just SENSITIVE.

Pain is a part of life. It motivates you to grow in understanding, compassion, and a myriad of other ways, and it is not personal.

Suffering comes when you personalize the pain. The story you tell yourself about the painful event, not the event itself, causes the suffering. When you focus on the story and don't allow the emotion to flow, it leads to stagnant emotional states such as resentment, shame, guilt, and fear.

In other words, if your interpretation is not health promoting, leading to a greater degree of effectiveness, understanding, connectedness, joy, love, peace or happiness, then it will produce suffering.

Once again, suffering is always created by the story you tell about the impersonal pain of life experience, not the pain itself.

Suffering is always chosen. Perhaps not consciously, but chosen just the same. I will talk more about that later.

Combativeness: (AKA: Screw you! You're not the boss of me!)

Let's just say I had a little problem with authority figures. My poor mom and dad were the first to get it from me, the rebellious reactionary!

I was often in a tug of war with others and myself. I constantly fought against what was happening-making it wrong. I was afraid, but it didn't show up that way, it showed up as irritation, anger, or absolute rage.

If someone did or said something that I didn't like I would resist or verbally attack. If circumstances, like the weather, didn't happen the way I wanted, I would get sullen and depressed.

I would say or think things like *'It's not fair! Why me? Why is this happening? What's wrong with me? What's wrong with people? Why is everyone else a douche bag? Why can't I trust anyone? People suck! People are never there for me! Why does this keep happening? Why do I always have to be the bigger person? God hates me! The devil made me do it! They rejected or abandon me! They hurt my feelings! They made me so mad! You're not the boss of me! Don't tell me what to do!'* The list goes on.

Oddly enough I got into the sport of boxing. I can remember one coach in particular told me *"To be a really good boxer, you have to have a lot of hate and anger driving you."* I remember saying to myself, "Well I guess I'm not going to be a very good boxer. I'm not full of anger and hate."

It's called denial.

I didn't think I was an angry person, and I had no idea that I was riddled with fear. The way I saw it, I was just a little rebellious.

Whatever is going on in life is just that, going on. It's passing through. But it can't pass if you fight it. As the saying goes, *"What you resist, persists."*

I nearly always got to have the fight I prepared for; and I was always prepared.

A word about Addictions

Addictions to substances, behaviors, and in some instances people are incredibly self-destructive as well as harmful to others. As an active alcoholic I engaged in risky behaviors and experienced car accidents, suicidal thoughts, emotional discomfort and on going physical sickness. I consistently put others and myself in harm's way.

I needed help beyond simply gaining information about my alcoholism. I needed assistance in the form of a twelve-step group to arrest the disease. I encourage anyone who is dealing with an addiction of any kind to avail themselves of one of the many groups, or other agencies whose purpose it is to empower people to arrest these deadly diseases.

I know mine nearly killed me.

You're worth the effort.

Wishful Thinking: (AKA: Fantasy Land Diary)

"Shoulda, Coulda, Woulda, all died when Didn't was born."
– Reverend Sheila McKeithen

My wishful thinking came in two flavors: wanting to be someone else, and wanting my past to be different.

I was practically a genius at dissecting what was "wrong" with my life and with me. From a very young age I just knew there was something not quite right about me. I sensed that I was born into the wrong family, the wrong era, the wrong race, certainly the wrong body.

I was too big, too white, too dumb, and too tall. My hair and eyes weren't the right color. I had crooked teeth and too many of them. I just didn't fit in anywhere.

If only I was like the short cute blonde girl in seventh grade. Maybe if I was a different race or ethnicity, then I'd be OK. Definitely if I had big boobs and was skinny then I'd be happy. Maybe one day, I'd become an adult; I'd have it all together; and grow long fingernails, surely then I'd be happy. I really just wanted to be someone else.

I did not accept myself. I mean I just knew I was a mistake. I believed that there was something so wrong with me that my only hope was for something outside of me to swoop down and make me different. There was a period of about thirteen years where I thought that magic something was alcohol, and it nearly killed me.

So how about wanting a different past? Like that's going to happen! As I mentioned before, I engaged in endless coulda, shoulda, woulda conversations with myself about past events. *"If I had just said this, or done that! Why did they do that? Why didn't they do this? It's not fair! It's not right! They shouldn't have done that! That was wrong!"* On and on, rehashing scenarios that were no more real than a movie projected on a screen.

The problem with wishful thinking is that it keeps you stuck in the past, or in fighting what is, both of which lead to suffering. There is no hope and no constructive action to be had.

No wonder suicide was a comforting thought to me. I would frequently think, *"If it gets too bad, I can off myself and make it look like an accident."*

Thankfully I don't think or live like that anymore.

Resignation and Detachment: (AKA: Screw it)

"I want to be left alone."
– Greta Garbo

Another pattern of the victim identity is becoming resigned and detached, which often leads to isolation. Let's look at what these words really mean.

To be **resigned** *is to accept something as inevitable, to give up deliberately; to quit.*

To be **detached** *is to withdraw, disengage, to separate, to be indifferent.*

When you are resigned, thinking you know how things are inevitably going to turn out; you give up, and deliberately quit.

Resignation thus effectively eliminates other possible outcomes to situations. You end up creating the very thing you say you do not want because you already "know" how "they" are or how "it" is going to go.

When you are detached, you become separate, isolated. How can you be consciously connected to yourself, God/Spirit or others when you are detached?

Detach with love? Impossible!

This is what the self-talk (thinking) of resignation and detachment sound like:

This is the way I am. This is the way I'll always be. Same old shit but a different day. That's it, I quit. I give up. I don't care anymore. I'm taking my ball and I'm going home. I won't play any more. I've been hurt for the last time. I'm through with you people, and these circumstances. They always screw me over. They never listen. They don't care about me, or what I'm dealing with. I'm done trying to make a difference. One person can't make a difference anyway. I don't care anymore. I think I'll just move to a cabin in the woods and get away from all of this. I'm going to just grind on until I can retire. Life is hard. Maybe there'll be something better on the other side. Maybe I could just go to jail or prison, and then I'll be taken care of.

By the time I said that little prayer, *"Dear God help me, I can't live like this,"* I had walled myself off in a prison of my own making and I didn't even know it. I was convinced that I knew who I was, what life was about, how people were and what was possible for me.

I had no dreams. I had no vision for my life, and no creative outlets. I had dropped my art and music years before. I really didn't think I could make much of a difference for others. Since I wasn't happy, how in the world was I going to do that for anyone else? I had a career and I wanted to feel like it was my *"calling,"* but I just wasn't feeling it in my heart.

My love life was a train wreck, constantly on an emotional roller coaster. The highs were thrilling, but the lows were crushing. I would go from bliss to emptiness, fear and depression and back all within a day. Drama, drama, drama and I saw no way to do it differently.

So screw it. I would give up and go get a pint of ice cream and some donuts. *"Well,"* I'd tell myself, *"It's better than a half rack of beer."*

It was so bleak, and I was so wrong. Maybe you are too.

Do you suppose that you are ready to give up giving up on yourself?

Regardless of how you currently think about yourself. Think again.

Take a minute to review your answers to the questions I suggested. What were the victim-identity patterns in your thinking and behaviors? Have you felt the way I described?

You are not these patterns. You're not.

Those behaviors are merely indicators of your current habits, nothing more.

You're doing great! Really. Being willing to look at any of this takes real courage. You are courageous!

Remember your awareness, your conscious awareness that you are engaging in victim identity behaviors gives you access to choosing to come from your authentic *Radical Self-Love, Child of God Identity.*

The next chapter is about doing just that.

Chapter 4 Summary

- When you choose the victim identity you do so because you're either unwilling to accept things as they are, or you're unwilling to take a doable action.
- Choosing the victim identity allows you to avoid taking responsibility for your life experiences.

- When in the victim identity you fight with, deny or run away from your life experiences.
- Recognizing your usual victim identity patterns is the first step to taking responsibility.
- Taking responsibility enables you to choose to come from your authentic *Radical Self-Love, Child of God Identity.*
- When engaging in *"people pleasing"* the likely purpose of your action is to gain validation from others rather than authentically expressing yourself.
- When engaging in *"manipulation and/or control"* the likely purpose of your action is to orchestrate people and situations in a way that you think will make you "feel" some particular way such as happy, content or loved.
- When engaging in "care-taking" the likely purpose of your action is to cause others to depend on you in order to feel needed and to earn their love.
- When engaging in *"hyper-responsibility"* the likely purpose of your action is to try to earn worthiness.
- When engaging in *"poll-taking"* the likely purpose of your action is to avoid taking responsibility for your life.
- When engaging in *"busyness"* the likely purpose of your action is to attempt to earn worthiness and avoid responsibility for your life.
- When engaging in *"complaining, judging and blaming"* the likely purpose of your action is to be *"right"* about others, situations, or yourself and avoid responsibility.
- When engaging in *"self-neglect and destructive behavior"* the likely purpose of your action is to avoid responsibility and exact revenge on others or yourself.
- When engaging in *"hypersensitivity"* the likely purpose of your action is to make others wrong and avoid responsibility for your life.
- When engaging in *"combativeness"* the likely purpose of your action is to avoid feeling fear and avoid responsibility for your life.
- Addictions are deadly, but can be arrested through the help of 12-step groups, programs, and other agencies.
- When engaging in *"wishful thinking"* the likely purpose of your action is to avoid feeling present emotions and avoid taking responsibility for your life.

- When engaging in *"resignation and detachment"* the likely purpose of your action is to be "right" about others or yourself and avoid taking responsibility for your life.

Chapter 5
Now that I can see the Drop of Sewage, how do I stop adding it to my glass?

"I can choose peace instead of this."
– A Course in Miracles

Congratulations for noticing that you are the one adding the victim-identity sewage to your glass of life.

What next? Dump the sewage tainted glass, clean it, and start over.

Begin again. Right now.

Choose something other than sewage to add to your glass of life. You can choose *Radical Self-Love*.

The remainder of this book provides detailed instructions and exercises that will teach you how to:

- **Recognize** when you are coming from the victim identity and drop it.
- **Clean up** any mess you've made while coming from the victim identity.
- **Choose** to come from your authentic *Radical Self-Love, Child of God Identity*.

Before you can truly begin again, you must be fully convinced that the victim identity sewage (victim beliefs, stories, and behaviors) that taint your life come from you.

The key to your freedom is being aware that you are the one creating the drop-of-sewage victim story. If you can distinguish it as just a *"story"* you created, and not the *"truth"* you can choose to stop creating it.

It may or may not be beneficial to distinguish the victim identity belief that generated the story. Either way, if you are willing to accept responsibility for telling the story that created your suffering, the suffering disappears. Without this acceptance, you will continue to fight, hate, resist, deny, or run from the truth.

YOU ARE THE SEWAGE BROKER IN YOUR LIFE

"However anxious you may be, you will not save yourself.

*The perfect men of old first had (what they wanted to do)
in themselves, and afterwards they found
(the response to it) in others."*
– Chuang Tzu

Engaging in a victim identity spree is like getting on a Ferris wheel in your mind. You are high, then low, spinning around and around going nowhere.

Acceptance allows you to get off the ride, to make a different choice. Total acceptance of yourself, and your life circumstances eliminates suffering. It is not the same as resignation or detachment.

To **accept** *simply means to understand or believe as true.*

Acceptance doesn't mean you have to like, approve of, or in any way acquiesce. Resignation and acquiescence lead to inaction or ineffective action of the same stripe. Acceptance leads to peaceful inaction or new effective action.

Once again, choice is a function of consciousness, or awareness. You cannot choose to get off the ride if you don't know you're on it.

ARE YOU READY TO STOP PIMP'N YOUR SOUL?

"There is nothing either good or bad, but thinking makes it so."
– Shakespeare

"We do not see things as they are; we see things as we are."
– Anonymous

"Nothing that enters one from outside can defile that person; but the things that come out from within are what defile."
– Mark 7:15

Often times you can catch yourself coming from the victim identity. Once you recognize it you can stop and choose to come from your *Radical Self-Love, Child of God Identity*. As with anything in life, the more you practice, the easier it gets.

At other times you may need help recognizing that you are coming from the victim identity.

Recognize *means to perceive clearly, realize, to acknowledge.*

Often times, those around you can perceive clearly what you don't acknowledge to yourself. Assistance can come from *God/Spirit*, and others. You can ask for help.

I often use the following prayer, *"Dear God/Spirit, please help me to see this (situation, thing, or person) differently."* I also have many trusted advisors; friends and family that I talk to when I suspect, but can't quite see how I am adding the victim identity drop of sewage to my life.

New view, new you!

It is your view or perception of things that determines your experience. When you change your perception of the things in your life, the things you perceive appear to change.

Habitual victim identity beliefs determined perceptions and thus your experiences.

For example, since I believed *"You can't trust people."* I was suspicious and fearful. The worst was yet to come! And it always did. It was not what was happening that created my experience, but my beliefs and subsequent perceptions.

53

You are in a constant dialogue with yourself about what is happening. You are not so much interacting with reality, but instead with your thoughts, beliefs, opinions, and perceptions of reality.

When you are upset about anything, and I do mean anything, it is because you are unwilling to accept things as they are. You've forgotten what you are, your authentic identity. You are rolling in the victim identity and telling a drop-of-sewage victim story about what happened. **You are creating the upset.**

When you are upset; it's always about you. You create the story that makes you suffer. An impersonal life circumstance occurs and you take it personally.

It really is that way.

That was a hard truth for me to believe.

"*Anything?*" I argued with the God/Spirit. "*But my brother died. Suddenly. It shouldn't have happened that way. He should still be here.*"

I believed that I had suffered greatly because of his untimely death.

Not so. I was not suffering because he died.

I was experiencing the pain of loss.

I was, and sometimes still am, sad because he's gone. I was missing him and still do.

I was suffering because I was telling myself that it shouldn't have happened that way. I should have been there. He was too young. He should have lived a long life and been here for me.

No acceptance. No peace.

My brother died at the age of 50, and I was not there. That happened.

I accepted it.

The acceptance of what was brought me peace of mind with what is.

Acceptance gave me a new perspective of his death and gave me access to creating a new set of beliefs about it. I created beliefs that continue to empower me.

The beliefs I created where: He is at peace. He did what he came to do and then he left. He watches over me and is always with me. He is helping me now.

Whether or not those new beliefs are "*true*" hardly matters. As Byron Katy says, "*If you're going to make up a story, and you will, make it a story that makes you feel good.*"

When the loss is a big one, it can take time to get to acceptance. Some call it the grieving process. Most of my spiritual growth has involved loss and grieving. Sometimes the loss is a person, a thing or an illusion. It is about letting go.

However, I have also experienced loss without grief. I have resigned from jobs, moved out of homes I loved and even lost relationships with complete and immediate acceptance and peace.

Regardless of the nature of the loss, it is possible to be powerful in dealing with any upset that occurs.

You can choose to take responsibility even with something as difficult as a death. Of course you can't stop someone from dying, but you can take responsibility for your response to it.

Taking total responsibility for everything that happens in your life gives you instant access to acceptance. It's just a powerful place to come from. If you choose to be responsible for your response, you can take actions that are healthy and life affirming. You can work through the loss, and the feelings in a healthy, authentic way that honors your loved one and yourself.

Rolling with the victim identity leaves you fighting, denying, hating or running from reality and leads to futility and suffering. Taking responsibility for your response gives you access to your *Radical Self-Love, Child of God Identity*.

CHAPTER 5 SUMMARY

- When you notice you've added sewage to your glass of life, dump the sewage tainted glass, clean it, and start over.
- Begin again.
- Beginning again requires recognizing when you are coming from the victim identity and dropping it; cleaning up any messes you've made; and choosing to come from your authentic *Radical Self-Love, Child of God Identity*.
- Distinguishing drop-of-sewage victim identity stories as *"stories"* eliminates suffering.
- Accepting life as it is brings peace.

- Recognition of sewage victim identity stories is some times difficult. You can ask God/Spirit, or trusted advisors for help.
- New view (perception), new you.
- Belief determines your perception, and your perception creates your experience. Thus if you change your beliefs, you change your experience of life.
- If you are upset it means you have forgotten that you are *Radical Self-Love, a Child of God*, and are playing the victim identity role.
- Upsets indicate a failure to accept a life circumstance as it is; you are taking the situation personally.
- Lack of acceptance results in you fighting, denying, hating or running from reality and leads to futility and suffering.
- Taking total responsibility for everything that happens in your life gives you instant access to acceptance.

CHAPTER 6
FREEDOM AIN'T FREE!

"If stupidity got us into this mess, why can't
stupidity get us out?"
– Will Rogers

"There is One Mind common to all people."
– Ralph Waldo Emerson

"The work is learning how to love you, all of you,
no matter what."
– Reverend Maggie Buck

Your only responsibility in this life is to *Radically Love* yourself. Now of course, if you have loved ones, pets, jobs, you are obliged to fulfill certain responsibilities. Being responsible is, after all a big part of *Radical Self-Love*. If you are being loving to you, you can't help but treat others with love, respect and dignity.

When you get angry with yourself or others, it is because you are afraid. You are believing a lie. It is likely that you are telling yourself a scary story. It feels terrifying and horrible because it is inconsistent with your *Radical Self-Love, Child of God Identity*. It is inauthentic and dishonest.

I used to bristle with antagonism if anyone used the *"G-word."* I could handle the idea of a Higher Power, but not God. I had all kinds of scary stories about *"God."* I believed God was a *"Big Daddy"* in the sky who was judging me, and waiting for me to screw up so he could punish me. Oh yeah and God was a he. I didn't think I could trust or relate to that kind of God.

I began to see that my reaction to that word was out of proportion and senseless- stupid really. So I did the work to free myself from those disempowering stories; I did a purge on God. (I will give instructions on how to purge in Chapter 9.)

I began to understand, and to know for myself, that the word *"God"* was just a word. I had made up a belief that God was judging and condemning based on what other people had told me.

I created new beliefs about God. At first I called it my Higher Power. The beliefs I created where: It loves me. It provides me comfort. It always has my back. It often works through other people to help me. It guides me if I ask.

I began to frequently experience my Higher Power as feelings of peace, love and joy inside of me. I was surprised to find that these experiences were not connected to any particular event. In other words, I would find myself feeling peaceful and joyous for no reason at all.

I could sense my Higher Power as a loving presence within me when I focused on my breathing. I could feel it as wonder when I looked at nature. I experienced it as a feeling, and a presence, both within and around me. I began to sense it in everything and everyone. I realized I no longer cared what I called it, and I no longer felt the need to define it beyond calling it the presence of Love.

If the word God still bothers you, try substituting another word like Love or Good, or Life, or Presence, or the Unknowable, or Jesus, or El Shaddai or Allah, or Ja, or Bahá or Buddha, or Spirit, or Your Soul, or the Universe, or the Big S Self, or Nothing, No Thing.

If you don't like any of those you could decide that the word GOD is an acronym for *Glorious Opportunities that are Doable*, or *Good Orderly Direction*, or *Grow Or Die.*

Does it really matter, what you call it? There is really only one ocean, but depending upon the shore you are standing on it's called the Atlantic or the Pacific, or the Indian or the Mediterranean or the Caribbean. I will continue to use *God/Spirit* in the text, but really, call it whatever you prefer, or nothing at all.

What's it gonna take to Radically Love You?

First you have to be willing to choose to Radically Love yourself. And/or you have to be willing to be willing to choose it.

OK. But what does that mean?

Willing *means inclined or favorably disposed in mind: ready; done, borne or accepted by choice or without reluctance.*

Choose *means to select freely and after consideration, to have a preference for.*

So to be willing is to choose something, to freely select it after you have weighed your options. After having considered your options you prefer to love yourself.

You may think you are not *"ready"* or you may believe you are *"reluctant"* to choose to love yourself. No problem. That is why I have said that you could be willing to be willing. You could be ready right now to be ready to do it.

You may think you do not know how to love yourself, and therefore you cannot choose it.

Not so.

I am merely asking you to choose it, to select it.

Think of me as your waitress. I hand you a menu, and you say to me, *"Miss Carol, Is the Radical Self-Love any good?"* And I say to you, *"Oh Sweetie, It's the best Love in the world. Try it you'll like it!"*

The rest of the book is about how to fulfill that choice.

There are three very important questions you must answer.

I invite you to get some paper and write out your responses to theses questions, and then say them out loud. (For example: I _____ (your name) am willing to choose...)

By writing these out and speaking them you are setting your intention and making a declaration. I will talk more about this powerful tool later.

Go on, get the paper, I'll wait.

1) Are you willing to choose to Radically Love yourself? If not, are you willing to be willing to choose it?
2) Are you willing to do the work necessary to take responsibility for your habits and your life as it is now?
3) Are you willing to do the work to develop new habits?

If you answered yes, you are well on your way. If not, then go on ahead, you're choosing to come from the victim identity. You are choosing to create suffering for yourself and others.

There's nothing *"wrong"* with continuing to choose the victim identity; it's common. It is the predominant choice of most people. No, I really mean it. There's nothing *"wrong"* with it, but it doesn't produce what most people really want in life.

Honestly most people don't even know that they are choosing the victim identity because it's so automatic. I chose it for years because I didn't know any better.

Most people want to love and be loved without conditions. Most people want to be their best self. Most people want to contribute and leave the world a better place than they found it. Most people want freedom, joy, peace and a world that works for all. (I would say all people but you'd probably want to argue!)

Here's where I draw a line in the sand.

You can't keep choosing the victim identity if you want love, freedom, joy, peace and a world that works for all. It just doesn't work. So if you still choose the victim identity, perhaps you need to convince yourself some more.

And then again, maybe you're ready to choose to Radically Love yourself and embrace your authentic *Radical Self-Love, Child of God Identity*. In any event, if you've read this far, a seed has been planted.

If you choose yes, the real work begins. Here's where the rubber meets the road. If not, again, perhaps this is a seed-planting book for you. No harm in reading further, is there?

RADICALLY LOVING YOU: THE SHORT CUT

I took the not so scenic long cut - lots of boxed canyons, blind alleys, ugly garbage dumps and the like. In my ample research trying what doesn't work, I have discovered what does work.

I suggest four tools that will enable you to drop the victim identity, Radically Love yourself and embody your authentic Radical Self-Love, Child of God Identity. They are:

1) Cultivate a Relationship with *God/Spirit*.
2) Understand and Apply Spiritual Law.
3) Practice The Presence of *God/Spirit*.
4) Train Your Mind.

Breaking the cycle of the victim identity allows you to take full responsibility for your created life. Learning how to *Radically Love Yourself*, is the blessed outcome and facilitator of the on-going process of stepping into your authentic *Radical Self-Love, Child of God Identity*.

Oh yes, and there is one more thing you have to give up if you choose to drop the victim identity.

You must give up having or hoping for a normal life.

Being a victim and complaining is normal. It's ordinary. It's usual. When you choose *Radical Self-Love*, you are choosing to be extraordinary, and to have a life beyond your wildest dreams! You are choosing your authentic *Radical Self-Love, Child of God Identity*.

In short you are choosing to be the very best person you can be.

Are you willing to be the very best person that you can be? Write the answer to that question down too. Declare it! Or not.

You don't have to know how to do that by the way. You can't know ahead of time. It means being new, every day. It's a process, not an event. *"What"* you are, *Radical Self-Love, a Child of God*, never changes. But your unique expression of that *"What,"* your unique *"Who You Are"* is ever expanding and creative! It is being the best you that you can be! Or not. You get to choose.

CULTIVATING A RELATIONSHIP WITH GOD/SPIRIT AND STEPPING INTO YOUR AUTHENTIC RADICAL SELF-LOVE, CHILD OF GOD IDENTITY

> "This above all: to thine own self be true,
> And it must follow, as the night the day,
> Thou canst not then be false to any man."
> – Shakespeare

"Beloved, we are God's children now."
– 1 John 3: 2

"God is love."
– 1 John 4: 8

You are Love and you are loved! You are the Light of the World!

You are Radical Self-Love, a precious Child of God, a Unique Spirit, or an individual Soul if you like. You are the only you there is; so you are the greatest!

All of these things are true, and you may know about these things, or even think you believe them. But are you true to those truths about you?

The proof is in the pudding. Chances are that if you have read this far, you don't really believe these things. Not really.

If you are not being true to who you really are, you will be false to others.

How DO I Love Myself Radically?

"The highest form of self-love is to be with, or observe oneself
without judgment."
– Panache Desai

"For the whole law is fulfilled in one statement, namely, love
your neighbor as yourself."
– Galatians 5: 14

To come from your authentic, *Radical Self-Love, Child of God Identity* means to Radically Love yourself. Let's look at what that really means.

Radical *means, of or relating to or proceeding from the root or origin, fundamental, a basic principle, foundation, extreme, marked by considerable departure from the usual, tending or disposed to make extreme changes in existing views, habits, and conditions.*

Love *is unselfish, loyal and benevolent concern for the good of another, to cherish, to hold dear, to thrive in, agape.*

Agape *means wide open, gaping, being in a state of wonder.*

Thus *Radical Self-Love* is that love of Self that comes from your root, fundamental being, and wholeness. It is the love that comes from your origin, and foundation and it is unusual, and extreme. It definitely is not normal or ordinary.

Radically Loving your Self is not selfish. It is authentic and natural. It is your birthright as *Radical Self-Love, a Child of God*. It is your mandate to be with yourself in an unselfish, loyal, benevolent, wide open, wonderful way that has you thrive!

You have a right to make extreme changes in your existing views, habits and the resulting conditions of your life. You were meant to live an extraordinarily loving life- to love yourself and others with agape love! You were meant to love in a wide-open way!

Selfish *means to be concerned excessively or exclusively with oneself; seeking or concentrating on one's own advantage, pleasure or well being without regards for others.*

Isn't that the perfect description of the victim identity?

I had been hurt too many times, so I locked my heart away in a protective prison so to speak. I believed I had been forgotten and abandoned by others, when in fact, if anything; I had forgotten and abandoned myself. I thought I was *"damaged goods."*

I had been waiting to fix myself, to change into someone good enough to be loved, and thus deserve to love myself. That is normal, conditional love. That is how our world teaches us to love. If I'm good, I receive love and approval, and if not, no love, and no approval.

That habitual way of thinking and believing was what needed *"healing."* I have experienced that kind of healing in my mind, and so can you.

Today, I get to choose to love myself abnormally, not just unconditionally, but ALL conditionally, the way *God/Spirit* loves me.

I choose to love myself for no reason at all, when I think I am at my absolute worst, when I am picking at myself, when I am full of judgment, shame and blame, anger, self-pity, fear, doubt or worry. I get to choose to love myself independent of my behaviors, emotional states, body sensations, external conditions, or the behaviors of other people.

It is totally without reason. It is UNREASONABLE.

If I behave lovingly towards myself, I will naturally do the same with others. *"Love your neighbor as yourself."* I have heard it said, that we all do that. That's why the world is in such a state. We don't love ourselves, and therefore we don't love others.

Your root, your origin is Pure Love, *God/Spirit*. You are fundamentally one with the One Love, *God/Spirit*. And that oneness, really means you're one with every other living thing. Thus, to *Radically Love your Self*, is to love ALL things. Do not let that scare you. It really means that no matter what it looks like, all things really love you too!

Imagine a world where *Radical Self-Love* and appreciation was the norm, and we all loved our neighbor as ourselves. It's possible you know! When we change, the world changes.

You can choose to believe that everyone loves you whether they know it or not, and that you love everyone whether you feel it or not. You can choose to behave in ways that are consistent with your *Radical Self-Love, Child of God Identity* no matter what!

You are your own laboratory in which you get to try the great experiment, or not.

I double dog dare you to try it. What do you have to lose?

HIGHER POWER ANYONE?

"Only the ego would want to get rid of the ego."
– Reverend Michael Bernard Beckwith

"Know God, know Peace. No God, No Peace."
– Anonymous

"Surely I, the Lord, do not change."
– Malachi 3:6

In order to come from your root, your origins, from what you really are, you must accept what you are. Accept that you are *Radical Self-Love, a Child of God*. Receive it, or be willing to receive it. Or be willing to be willing to receive it.

There is simply no way around it. You are an eternal being, *Radical Self-Love, a Child of God*. It is your Identity. It is what you are. As I've said, when you roll in the victim identity it is because you have forgotten what you are and where you come from.

You may already have a *God/Spirit* of your understanding, if so, that's fantastic. The questions I have for you are: How does your understanding work for you? Do you trust this power? Do you have a relationship with it? Do you know it, or merely know about it?

If you don't have an understanding of *God/Spirit* or if you don't trust or have a relationship with *God/Spirit*, you can begin again right now.

Perhaps you've been waiting for *God/Spirit* to do something for you, or to you, so that you can have a better life, hear this- *God/Spirit* is waiting on you!

Hear me now! *God/Spirit* is waiting on you to receive what has already been given. Your prayer does not change *God/Spirit*, it changes your willingness to receive; your availability to all that has already been given to you.

The only real need you have, in any given moment, is to be the very best version of yourself that you can be. You are an ever expanding, always growing, unfolding idea in the mind of *God/Spirit*. You are *Radical Self-Love, a Child of God*.

God/Spirit already gave you everything you need to fully express your unique and unqualified genius, your talents and gifts. What you need is already in you! Get it?

The love you seek is within you now.

You are full of it- full of *Radical Self-Love*. You are *Radical Self-Love, a Child of God*, and so you can't help it, you need to uniquely express the Love that you are. That is the only real need that you have!

I was told early in this adventure, that I could have any *God/Spirit* I wanted. The only requirements were that it had to be something greater than my little "s" self, and I had to be willing to cultivate a dependence upon it. Or as another of my mentors once told me, *"You can make up any God/Spirit you want as long as you're not it."*

I knew my little "s" self/ego wasn't cutting it. I loved the idea that my ego was really just a protective personality, or my reptilian survival oriented brain patterns. It is not evil, or bad. I don't need to get rid of it, however it is not what I want running the show.

It's not about getting rid of any part of you that is real. And that requires more than mere self-knowledge, it requires surrender-letting go and allowing something sacred to take hold of you.

There is a difference between knowing about *God/Spirit*, and knowing *God/Spirit*.

When you are disassociated from your true Identity, you're ego, with its habitual victim-identity patterns, will call the shots. And that is not remotely pleasant, for you or those around you.

Please, for the love of God/Spirit get it! YOU, yes YOU, are so very important!

You are here to help others with your unique gifts, talents and capacities. If you don't develop them no one will. You are here to make the difference you alone can make. By playing small and safe you aren't just *"hurting"* yourself. You are impacting all those for whom you can make a difference, including yourself.

When you are connected to *God/Spirit*, you have the ability to be responsible. You have response ability, rather than reactivity. You can choose. You can come from a very different set of beliefs based on a direct contact and dependence on the Power, and the Presence of *God/Spirit*.

Thomas Edison once gave a lecture about electricity. Afterwards a woman asked, *"Mr. Edison, what is electricity?"* He is said to have replied, *"My dear, electricity is, use it."*

God/Spirit is- Use it. Or, rather, let it work for, in, through and as you. Let it use you to help others and yourself.

Think of it this way, an electrical appliance works to its maximum potential when it is plugged in. You are like that too. A lamp can act as a paperweight or something else, but it is most useful when it is plugged in and turned on.

When you are plugged in and turned on you naturally shine the light that is your unique expression of the power flowing through you. The divine aspect of who you are is ever seeking to express itself in and through and as you.

I invite you to give it permission to do so.

Say if you will, *"I give God/Spirit permission to work in and through and as me to express the very best me that I can be."*

The power and presence is waiting your permission. It is as if we have a garden hose that is connected to a vast and infinite aquifer. We can if we wish stand on the hose and prevent the water from flowing, or we can get off the hose drink freely and water our garden.

Being consciously connected to *God/Spirit* is like that.

Aren't you thirsty to be you and share your gifts- to grow your garden so others can share in the gift that is you?

DESIGN A GOD/SPIRIT

"Draw near to God and he will draw near to you."
– James 4: 8

"This is God your Lord: All power is His: But the gods ye call on besides Him have no power over the husk of a date stone!"
– The Koran

If you don't have a *God/Spirit*, or the one you've got doesn't work for you, you can as I did, choose one that works for you.

By the time I said that little prayer, *"Please God help me I can't live like this,"* I was convinced that *God/Spirit* hated me, and that I was going to hell for sure. I had done too many bad things and I was sure *God/Spirit* was punishing me, which I was sure I deserved.

I began with three simple practices. Let me describe to you how I began and guide you to do likewise.

The first thing I did was to list all of the qualities I would like *God/Spirit* to have. My list of qualities included: loving, kind, gentle, forgiving, helpful, comforting, merciful, understanding and dependable. That was enough to begin.

I invite you to get some paper and create your own list. Even if you have a relationship with *God/Spirit*, I invite you to do the exercise anyway. You may discover something new for yourself. Remember *God/Spirit* is infinite, so perhaps you could set aside what you think you already *"know"* such that you could have a new experience with *God/Spirit.*

Now that you have a list of qualities of *God/Spirit*, I suggest you write them on a post-it note or two and place them where you will see them often. Remind your self that you are going to be open to experiencing *God/Spirit* and yourself as these qualities.

The second thing I did was to start praying. At first I simply asked for help, and it grew from there. Try it now if you will. Try three simple prayers, or intentions if you dislike the word prayer.

- *Please help me to be my best self today.*
- *Thank you for helping me.*
- *Please help me to know you and myself as _____. (State a quality from your God/Spirit list.)*

You can use these prayers through out the day. I was told that if I was having a *"bad"* day, I could start it over any time. These simple prayers can be used to begin again. Start the day over. Reset yourself. You can interrupt the momentum of habitual victim identity thinking in just that way.

I am asking you to try this for just one day, or if that is too much, try it for one hour. See for yourself that you can choose to consciously connect to *God/Spirit*.

The third thing I did was to pay attention to my thinking. My thinking was extremely negative and undisciplined. I was told to use my attention to focus my thinking constructively. I started using affirmations.

Frequent repetition of truth is called AFFIRMATION.

An **affirmation** *is a positive assertion, a solemn declaration. To affirm is to make firm, validate, confirm, to assert as valid.*

I memorized and repeated the serenity prayer, and several affirmations.

Remember, a belief is a habit of thought. Habits are only acquired through frequent repetition. The victim identity is a set of habitual beliefs. You must create new habitual beliefs that are consistent with your *Radically Self-Love, Child of God Identity* or you will automatically revert back to the victim identity.

I used to hate my body. I told myself stories that I was too tall, too white, my hands were too big, my boobs were too small, and I didn't think I was pretty enough. I believed all of that.

Additionally, I had severe injuries from a car accident. Amongst other injuries, I had several prolapsed discs and three fractured vertebrae. The fracture sites stuck out like a dorsal fin, and I was in almost constant pain. I routinely took upwards of nine, 200 mg ibuprofen to make it through the day.

Had I continued to hate my body and believe that it would never heal, it wouldn't have. In fact it probably would have gotten worse. That is the *"normal"* prognosis for those kinds of injuries.

One day I sat across from my mentor Hedi (sic) and she asked me to stroke my arm and say, *"Thank you for this healthy vessel."* I couldn't finish the sentence without bursting into tears.

I wrote about my relationship with my body, I did a purge (I'll give directions on how to do this in Chapter 9.). I discovered that I believed that my body wasn't good enough. But more importantly, I saw that neither that belief, nor the stories were the truth; I had made them up.

I was astonished! If that belief and those stories weren't true, then what was? What did I want to believe about my body? What story did I want to tell? What did I want to create?

I began to use affirmations to practice a new set of beliefs. I started with some Louise Hay affirmations and tailored them to fit me. Here they are:

I am young beautiful and healthy; my body knows it and shows it. My spine is straight and curves in all the right places. I love my titties, I love my ass, I love my skin; I love my face; I love my body; I love myself. I am entitled to miracles; I rest in God.

At first I had a hard time saying the affirmations, and an even harder time remembering them, but I persisted. It didn't take long before I had a completely different relationship with my body.

I started taking care of my body in ways I hadn't before. I started stretching and found new exercises that seem to really help my back. I started drinking a lot more water as well as green smoothies with ground flax seed for breakfast. My sugar intake plummeted, and I stopped drinking diet soda. I started to appreciate my body's strength and resiliency. I developed the habit of praising and thanking it for working well and healing.

I would run around Lake Merritt in Oakland and repeat my affirmations over and over. Whenever I noticed my mind chattering negatively, I would redirect it by using these affirmations. Not that I believed them, I didn't, not at first. But the more I said them, the easier they were to say. I still use them, and I've expanded on them.

When you say or think an affirmation and it is easy to say, you are likely affirming a belief that you already hold.

When you say or think an affirmation and it is difficult to say, or you have trouble remembering it, you are likely affirming a belief that you DO NOT yet believe.

THIS IS VERY EXCITING!

If you persist, you will be engaging in the deep practice necessary for the affirmation to become a belief!

When a previously inactive belief becomes activated, extraordinary things begin to happen!

Today, I love and appreciate my body! I take care of it.

I rarely take pain medication anymore because I'm rarely in pain. The fracture sites are continuing to move back into their normal position. I now have a normal curve in my lower back that was not there for over 20 years. I fully expect a complete healing. My doctors, physical therapist and others told me these fractures would never move.

The movement of these fractures and the healing of my back began approximately 10 years after the accident. Why not before? I did not heal before because I did not believe that it was possible. The healing occurred first in my mind, my thinking, and my beliefs.

When a belief changes, your view changes, and when your view changes, you begin to take different actions and so different results are possible.

I began to love my body, and believe that it could heal. I found healers that helped me. I have worked with personal trainers, gone to chiropractors, acupuncturists, hypnotherapists, sound therapists, and Rolfers. I continue to exercise, stretch, and eat highly nutritious foods. I became a vegetarian. I continue to gain in strength and flexibility as I get older, and that is not normal, particularly given my history.

The on going healing that I am experiencing is extraordinary, in fact miraculous!

New view, new you!

Here are some examples of powerful affirmations that you can choose to practice. If you don't care for these, make up your own.

Affirmations

- I am a Child of *God/Spirit*: Perfect, Whole, and Complete.
- *God/Spirit* wants me to be Happy, Joyous and Free.
- It is *God/Spirit*'s good pleasure to give me the kingdom.
- I am on Purpose, with a Purpose.
- *God/Spirit* is always with me, even when I don't feel it.
- All is well.
- Thank you.
- I love you _____ (say your own name.)
- I am the Greatest, because there's only one of me.
- I am God/Spirits' Gift to the world.
- With *God/Spirit*, all things are possible.
- *God/Spirit* can make a way out of no way.
- I am the light of the world.
- *God/Spirit* is here with me now.
- *God/Spirit* is closer than my breath, nearer than hands and feet.
- There are no problems, only opportunities.
- Everything is just the way it's supposed to be.
- I am always in the right place at the right time.
- I am floating in an ocean of devotion.
- I am wanted, needed and loved.
- The Universe is incomplete without me.
- Everything is working together for my good.
- I am Divinely supported.
- I am calm, clear, and confident.
- I am guided, guarded, protected and directed in all ways, and always.
- Everything and everyone is on my side even if it doesn't seem like it.
- This _____ (name the experience or condition) may be a fact, but it is not the truth of what and who I am.
- Thank you for bringing into my awareness that which I need to release.
- I am releasing all resistance now.
- I am willing to change. I am willing to release all resistance to change.
- I am willing, I am available, I am open to the highest good now.
- There is always enough because I am enough.
- I am wanted, needed, loved and appreciated.

- I love and appreciate myself.
- I forgive others, I forgive myself and I am forgiven.
- I am wholly loveable and wholly loving.
- I am wholly forgivable and wholly forgiving.

You can start using affirmations immediately. I invite you to choose one from the list that appeals to you or make up one of your own. Remember, affirmations are written and said in present tense, *"I am"* not *"I will be."* You are affirming truth now, not in the future. After all it is always now. There is never a time when it is not now.

Next, write the affirmation on a note card, and several sticky notes. Keep the note card in your pocket and post the sticky notes on your mirror, the dashboard of your car or other locations that will remind you to say the affirmation.

Try to say the affirmation at least twice an hour through out your day. If you can't say it out loud, think it. I would also suggest that you use it as one of your morning and evening intentions, which I will cover in Chapter 8.

If you find that you are extremely resistant to the affirmation you have chosen, and you find yourself denying it instead, you may need to do a purge about the subject before you use affirmations. I give directions in Chapter 9 for how to do a purge.

In any event affirmations can quickly redirect you attention when you find yourself in victim identity thinking. I use prayer and affirmation frequently. When I do this it is easier to stay present and loving.

Chapter 6 Summary

- Your only responsibility in this life is to *Radically Love* yourself.
- When you engage in *Radical Self-Love*, you naturally fulfill your responsibilities to others and yourself.
- *"God"* is just a convenient word used to describe your origins. It's just a word. Use whatever you prefer.
- In order to *Radically Love* yourself, you must choose or be willing to choose your authentic *Radical Self-Love, Child of God Identity.*

- In order to *Radically Love* yourself, you must be willing to do the work necessary to take responsibility for your habits and your life as it is now.
- In order to *Radically Love* yourself, you must be willing to do the work to develop new habits.
- There are four tools that can assist you in *Radically Loving* yourself and choosing your authentic *Radical Self-Love, Child of God Identity.*
    - Cultivate a Relationship with God/Spirit
    - Understand and Apply Spiritual Law
    - Practice The Presence of God/Spirit
    - Train Your Mind
- You must give up the hope of having a *"normal"* life if you choose your authentic *Radical Self-Love, Child of God Identity.*
- Radically loving yourself means you treat yourself in a loving manner, no matter what.
- Most people learn to love conditionally. Most people do *"Love your neighbor as yourself,"* which is to say, they don't.
- You are an eternal being, *Radical Self-Love, a Child of God.* It is your Identity.
- *God/Spirit* already gave you everything you need to fully express your unique and unqualified genius, your talents and gifts. It's in you. It is you.
- When you are not connected to *God/Spirit* you are unlikely to remember what you are, and will likely come from the victim identity.
- You can design and develop a relationship with a *God/Spirit* that works for you.
- Affirmations are truth statements.
- Affirmations are a tool to direct your thoughts towards creating beliefs that are consistent with your authentic *Radical Self-Love, Child of God Identity.*
- A belief is just a thought that you think habitually.
- It is easy to affirm a belief that you already hold.
- It is difficult to affirm a belief that you DO NOT yet hold.
- Creating a new belief results in new and unexpected results.
- Affirmations are written as "I am" statements followed by the belief you desire to hold.

Chapter 7
Understanding and Applying Spiritual Law- Word!

"All is Love, yet all is Law."
– Robert Browning

"But I say to you, love your enemies, and pray for those who
persecute you, that you may be children of your heavenly Father,
for he makes his sun rise on the bad and the good and causes rain
to fall on the just and the unjust."
– Matthew 5:44

"The reason we do not know the power of our word, is that we've
forgotten what we've said."
– Reverend Barbara King

My life was a mess because I was breaking all the rules and laws of life. My thinking was chaotic and I believed things that were not true. As a consequence, my behavior was chaotic and so I created chaos everywhere I went.

Every person has the capacity to have an intimate personal and loving relationship with *God/Spirit*; however, the care of *God/Spirit* is impersonal. *God/Spirit* cares for you via the Spiritual Laws- justice without judgment.

If you are anything like I was, you have no idea what I mean by the term "*Spiritual Laws.*" No worries. I'll break it down for you.

Your "*word*" is what you say or think about yourself, others and life.

So what?

Your life is a demonstration of your "*word*," that's what!

The things you say and think repetitively become your beliefs. You have the power to name things in your life. You can name it all "*good*", or you can name it all "*bad*," and so goes your experience.

Your "*word*" is also how you know yourself. How you define yourself. When you talk about yourself you say "*I am this.*" or "*I am that.*" When you say "*I am,*" you are invoking the Spiritual Laws of creation because you are declaring what you believe, and so goes your experience. If you understand that, you will be very careful about how you finish the sentence "I am..."

I am tired. I am lonely. I am broken. Or I am grateful. I am vigorous. I am wonderful! Which do you prefer to create?

I started to become aware of my habitual words and thoughts, including those about myself. I was astonished by how frequently they were negative and critical. If anyone else had talked to me that way, I wouldn't have stood for it.

Additionally, your "*word*" is the promise that you make. It is the one thing that no one can take from you, and the one thing no one can give for you.

When you give your "*word*" to another and/or yourself, and you keep it, or honor it you feel whole. When you don't you don't.

In a nutshell, keeping your "*word*" means to keep the promises you have made (including the promises you've made to yourself). It means that you do what you said you would do, when you said you would do it.

If you cannot keep your "*word*" you can still honor it. Honoring your "*word*" means communicating to the person to whom the promise was made that you are not going to keep your promise, and then making a new promise.

For example, I might promise to pick you up at 5 pm. If I do so, I have kept my "*word*." If I am running late, and call to let you know that I will be 5 minutes late, I have honored my "*word*." I honor my word by taking responsibility. I have come from my *Radical Self-Love, Child of God Identity*.

On the other hand if I do not communicate, arriving 5 minutes late, I have neither kept nor honored my word. I might make excuses or get defensive and angry if you mention that I was late. I may speed and feel irritable and anxious, and may accuse you of being rigid. I may blame you and complain about all of the times that you have been late. I will probably have disempowering thoughts about myself. I might tell myself that I suck, or that I'm a lame ass friend. I may feel embarrassed and ashamed. I have allowed the victim identity to take over.

Thus when you do not keep or honor your *"word"* you experience yourself as the victim identity and often create conflict with others.

You create your life with your *"word."* You create your experience of yourself with your *"word."*

It's the law. You experience yourself as your *"word."*

GRAVITY IS

"Sit down and shut up. You are drunk and this is
the edge of the roof."
– Rumi

Gravity is. It is a physical law. If you hold a pencil out in front of you and let it go, it will automatically fall to the ground. It will not fall up no matter how much you want it to, or think it should, or how much it hurts your feelings that it falls to the floor.

It's not personal.

If you stand on a chair and step off you are coming down. If you get up on the roof and step off you are coming down harder, and you might break your leg. The law of gravity is not trying to hurt you. It could give a rip. It's just not harmonious for you to step off a roof.

Gravity is.

HIT ME! ARE YOU ASKING FOR IT?

Ignorance of the Law does not exempt you from the consequences. Cause and effect is the most basic Law. In essence, once you have made a choice, the consequences of your choice occur whether you like it or not.

You cannot choose to plant a radish seed and expect corn to grow instead. You cannot sit on the couch watching television and expect that the mess you made in the kitchen will magically disappear. Equally, if you are kind and loving, you create kind and loving results.

There are no problems in Life. Life just is. Gravity just is. Gravity does not have a problem with you, or an opinion about anything you do concerning it. It would be a problem if you had to force the pencil to the ground and somehow keep it there, but no, it's automatic. It is the same way with *Spiritual Law*. It is likewise impersonal.

When I discovered that there were *Spiritual Laws* I started reading sacred texts and nearly any metaphysical book I could get my hands on. I wanted to know what these Laws were, and how to get into harmony with them. Charles would remind me, *"Carol, everything is harmonious, just don't fuck it up."* Well, I practically had a PhD in fucking up. I nearly always chose the path of most resistance.

LOOKING FOR DEMONSTRATIONS

> "Faith is the realization of what is hoped for, the evidence of
> things not seen."
> – Hebrews 11:1

Faith *means a firm belief in something for which there is no proof.*

I had no faith that *God/Spirit* would work in my life. Well, actually, I was sure *God/Spirit* was out to get me. I needed to be shown. I was like Thomas; I wanted to stick my finger in the nail prints before I could believe that *God/Spirit* would care for me. I needed *"evidence."* And evidence is just what I got. I got to see the *"substance"* of the things I was hoping for right there in my very own life.

Let me explain.

I started to look for demonstrations of the laws working in my life. I was on a hunt to notice how *God/Spirit* was caring for me always, and in all ways.

Demonstration *means conclusive evidence, or proof.*

I wanted to have proof, evidence that these laws really worked. I needed to make that connection for myself. I started with simple things. I noticed that harmonious actions produced harmonious results.

I noticed that when I paid my bills first, and then spent money on other things, I was not anxious and worried. I noticed that when I did my dishes consistently, that my kitchen stayed clean, and I felt less scattered. I noticed that when I prayed, and asked for help, I instantly felt better on the inside. Something happened in me.

I noticed that inharmonious actions likewise produce inharmonious results. I saw that when I procrastinated, I felt fearful and irritable. When I overworked and didn't get enough rest I would engage in self-destructive compulsive behaviors like binge eating my way through a bag of candy and a pint of frozen yogurt. When I gossiped, or lied, or was judgmental or didn't keep my word I felt small, weak, unhappy, guilty and full of shame.

Additionally, weird unaccountably positive things started happening on the outside, in my life circumstances-coincidences.

What's that mean?

Coincidence *is the occurrence of events that happen at the same time by accident but seem to have some connection, or to correspond in nature.*

Bottom line- miracles started happening in my life. As if by accident, people would call at just the right time, and have the answer to a *"problem"* I was dealing with. Songs on the radio, billboards, and snatches of conversations I was eavesdropping on seem to correspond with the answers to questions I had. It seemed that all of life was speaking words of comfort, guidance and assurance to me. It was unbelievable!

In this way, I began to develop faith and trust in *God/Spirit*. I was having personal and intimate experiences of this Presence working in my life. I prayed, and something happened in and around me. The care of *God/Spirit* went from being an idea to being an experience. No one could tell me different.

Little by little I started connecting the dots. Demonstrations (effect), come from my actions, and my actions are a direct match to my beliefs (cause).

I saw for the first time HOW I was creating my life through the use of these *Spiritual Laws*. It took me a long time to finally see what the fundamental identity issue was. Oh well. As I've said, I've taken the long cut. You can, if you wish, take a short cut.

THE LAWS- LINE UP!

"Watch your thoughts, they become words;
watch your words, they become actions;
watch your actions, they become habits;
watch your habits, they become character;
watch your character, for it becomes your destiny."
– Frank Outlaw

Through much study and trial and error, I have discovered the following *Spiritual Laws*. This is by no means a comprehensive list or explanation of *Spiritual Laws*. It is likely that I barely scratch the surface of understanding them. I strive to stay in alignment with these *Spiritual Laws* because when I do I have a bliss-filled, wonderful, free flowing, service oriented life.

Life is delicious!

I have nicknames for some of the *Spiritual Laws*. This is not an academic treaty; it is a personal testimony. Call them what you will, it hardly matters as long as you behave in ways that produce harmony, peace, love and joy.

No doubt some of you may disagree with my explanation-that's fine. I share my experience. Their validity is not something that I need to prove to you. I have demonstrated their power in my life. In fact, you can't take my word for it. You have to apply them yourself, for yourself. Here goes...

SPIRITUAL LAW- GET IN ALIGN!

The Law of Life

> "Do not be afraid any longer little flock; for your Father is
> pleased to give you the kingdom."
> – Luke 12:32

> "Life is supposed to be good for you. You live, whether you know
> it or not, as the full recipients of a hurricane of grace that is
> flowing towards you at all times in answer to all that you have
> been asking for."
> – Abrahams-Hicks

The **Law of Life** says that there is infinite good and God/Spirit wants to give it to you.

Life is always for you and never against you. There is no lack. There is infinite grace always available to you.

So what is grace?

Grace *is unmerited Divine assistance, an act of kindness, compassion, clemency, mercy, reprieve and pardon; a blessing or a fortunate circumstance coming from God/Spirit; it is a privilege, or special favor.*

Cool! Then how come I don't manifest everything I want? What gives?

Your personal application of the remaining *Spiritual Laws*, dictates your personal use of the Law of Life. In other words, you can limit your experience of the limitless good that is available to you.

The Law of Mind in Action or the Law of Experience

> "Let it be done for you according to your faith."
> – Matthew: 9:29

> "You do not believe what you see; you see what you believe."
> – Anonymous

The **Law of Mind in Action** is It is done unto you, AS you believe.

This is the granddaddy of them all. As I've mentioned earlier, this is how you create your personal law.

Your beliefs govern how you use or misuse all of the remaining *Spiritual Laws*.

Did you hear that? It's really, really important. I'll say it again.

Your beliefs govern how you use or misuse all of the remaining *Spiritual Laws*.

It is how you create your life experiences. Your habitual beliefs set everything else in motion. They dictate your views, your perceptions, your emotions, your actions and reactions to people and events.

When your personal law is that you are *Radical Self Love, a Child of God*, the *Spiritual Laws* produce harmony and joy automatically. When your personal law is that you are a victim, the *Spiritual Laws* produces chaos and misery automatically. Remember, it's like gravity, automatic and impersonal.

The Law of Karma

The **Law of Karma** is that what you put out in the world, you get back.

This is also known as the Law of Cause and Effect, or *"What comes around, goes around."* My experience of Karma is that it always works; whatever you put out, you get back. As you give so shall you receive, and always without delay.

If you are being loving towards another, you get the first dose of that love. If you are being judgmental, you get the first dose of judgment. You have to be, who you are being. It is immediate.

You do not have to wait for the consequences of who you are being, although often there are additional consequences that are delayed. You always get the real-time result of you being you.

One time I called Wells, another of my mentors, in tears about this man I was dating. Someone had told me something he had said, and I was UPSET!

She stopped me before I could finish the story and said with obvious distaste, *"You weren't...listening to gossip? Were you? Well I guess you're getting what you get."* And then, she told me to meditate on that and hung up! *"My God!"* I thought, *"What a cold-hearted bitch!"* But she was right.

I was gossiping. I was being fearful, suspicious and unloving. I got to experience all of that immediately, and I began to make up stories about my boyfriend that generated more fear, and suspicion. I had created suffering for myself. It was a vicious cycle.

The Law of Multiplicity

"Stop judging and you will not be judged. Stop condemning and you will not be condemned. Forgive and you will be forgiven. Give and gifts will be given to you: a good measure, packed together, shaken down, and overflowing, will be poured into your lap. For the measure with which you measure will in return be measured out to you."
– Luke 6: 37-38

The **Law of Multiplicity** is that you get back what you put out, amplified, or in an exaggerated fashion.

Some call this the Law of Generosity, the Law of Give and Take or the Golden Rule. *"Do unto others, as you would have them do unto you."*

Once again, it is done unto you AS you believe. So if you believe in judgment and condemnation, guess who's inviting the *Spiritual Laws* to bring it on? Hit me again, will you? But, if you choose to be generous, kind and grateful, the *Spiritual Laws* will send you more of that, amplified!

The choice is yours.

Nature is a great example of this. If you plant a single tomato seed, that seed is multiplied. One seed produces a plant. That one plant in turn produces a plethora of seeds. When you give, you are the first recipient. If you are generous, generosity becomes part of your personal law. You believe it, thus you experience it.

The Law of Focus

The **Law of Focus** is that whatever you focus on in life grows bigger.

This is also known as the Law of Attraction, or the Law of Increase. If you are irritated, you will attract more things to be irritated about. Everything will bug you. If you focus on what's seems good to you, you will see more good! Everything will appear lovable and lovely! Make your choice wisely!

If you focus on how much you love your partner, you will notice their lovable qualities. You won't see that they chew with their mouth open, or squeeze the toothpaste tube in the *"wrong"* way. You will see how generous, kind and funny they can be. You will see their quirks and love that about them too. It's all in your view-what you are choosing to focus on.

I got a rather mundane, but powerful demonstration of this when I became interested in buying a Ford Ranger pick-up. All of the sudden I saw Ford Ranger pick-ups everywhere. What? Where did they all come from? They were always there. I just wasn't looking for them. Try it yourself with something simple, like a pick-up. Prove it to yourself.

The Law of Asking

> *"Ask and you will receive; seek and you will find; knock and the door will be opened to you."*
> – Luke 11:9

The **Law of Asking** is that if you ask you will be given, and if you seek, you will find what you are looking for; and if you don't, you won't.

However, remember the law only knows what you are asking for by what you focus your attention on. The law does not know no. It always says yes.

Let me say that again. **The law does not know no. It always says yes.**

Give yourself a moment to ponder that before continuing.

If you are focused on *"I don't want to be late,"* the law only knows that you focus is on being late. You will likely draw into your experience red lights and slow traffic. If instead you focus on *"I want to be on time,"* the law knows that your focus is on being on time. You will likely draw into your experience green lights and smooth traffic. If your focus flits back and forth between those two opposing thoughts, you will get mixed results.

I was told that *God/Spirit* is the consummate gentleman or gentlewoman; he/she does not go where not invited. If you ask for help, you'll get it, and if you don't you won't. If you are looking for answers, you get them, if not, then not.

My only caveat is that you ask empowering questions, harmonious questions. I'll address asking powerful questions in Chapter 8.

So I started asking. I started praying for help, and I started asking for Divine Guidance. I asked for awareness. I requested that I become aware of when my thinking was harmonious, and when it wasn't. I became a seeker. I wanted to know what was missing so I could get it and fix myself.

In my searching, I discovered something really startling.

I discovered that I already had everything I needed; and it was in me. All I really needed was to be myself, my best self.

At first I knew it intellectually, as an idea. It took practice to believe it and more practice to know it in my heart. I continue to practice. I will give specific instructions on the practices I use in the next several chapters.

My asking transformed from asking to get things and manipulate people and circumstances to asking for assistance in developing specific qualities. I asked for help in developing my capacity to be loving, grateful and kind.

I began to see the difference between my wants and my needs. I began to grasp that I was meant to express unique gifts and talents.

It dawned on me that I didn't need to be better than anyone else, I needed to better than the *"me"* I was yesterday. I began to slowly but surely ask for what I really needed- to express my authentic *Radical Self-Love, Child of God Identity* in my unique way.

The Law of Opposites

I like to call this Law, the Law of "Be careful what you pray for, you just might get it!"

The **Law of Opposites** responds when you ask for something. It will attract the perfect environment for you to develop the quality you need in order to create what you are asking for. Often the environment appears to be the exact opposite condition.

The perfect environment and people will be attracted, such that you will have to grow in just that way. The un-manifest potential of that quality within you, by necessity, will emerge.

When I was seventeen I went on a senior retreat and I identified the one quality that I knew I needed to develop the most was patience. I had none, so that is what I prayed for, patience.

I was a high school teacher for twenty-six years, in both inner city Oakland, California and in the Hillyard neighborhood of Spokane, Washington. I had ample opportunity to develop and practice patience in those environments! It has worked.

You cannot see a candle flame in full sunlight. It radiates its full potential in a dark room. You are like that.

When you desire to create love, you may find yourself in environments seemingly devoid of love. You become the love that is "missing." You get to shine in the dark places of your life. When you behave lovingly, and nothing and no one can stop you, you know yourself to *be love*.

The Law of Gratitude and Appreciation

The **Law of Gratitude and Appreciation** says that what you appreciate gets bigger.

The Law says that *"thank you"* is a multiplier. It amplifies whatever it is attached to.

It is really a specific application of the law of focus, or attraction. I designated it as a separate law because it is so powerful.

The vibration of gratitude and appreciation is so empowering to human beings that it can lift and shift a mood and mind set faster than nearly anything else. It can make a bad situation good and a good situation great. And it is so easy to access!

The Law says that if you are grateful, you will attract more things, people and circumstances for which to be grateful.

Try this simple exercise for the next two weeks.

When you wake up, before you get out of bed practice being grateful. Say out loud at least 5 times each of the following.

- Thank you for _____. (The names of 5 specific persons or animals.)
- Thank you for _____. (5 specific other blessings.)
- Thank you for _____. (5 specific challenges.)

- Thank you for _____. (5 specific gifts or talents you have.)
- Thank you! (5 times for nothing at all.)
- Thank you for this day!

Let me give you an example so you really get this.

- Thank you for mom. Thank you for Janet. Thank you for Ron. Thank you for Jane. Thank you for Trisha.
- Thank you for my bed. Thank you for a great night sleep. Thank you for coffee. Thank you for waking me up this morning. Thank you for the sun.
- Thank you for this soreness in my shoulder. Thank you for the stain I can't get out of my work apron. Thank you that I ate dessert twice last night. Thank you for the judgment I have about eating dessert twice. Thank you for the thoughts that I have more to do than I can get done today.
- Thank you for my willingness. Thank you for my ability to feel and be compassionate. Thank you for my physical strength. Thank you for my ability to work hard. Thank you for my ability to write.
- Thank you! Thank you! Thank you! Thank you! Thank you!
- Thank you for this day!

When you practice this exercise, see if you can feel the energy of gratitude in your heart. If you can't, then this is deep practice! It simply means that you are right now developing a habit of gratitude.

Try the gratitude exercise right now, don't wait. I'll wait for you to do it.

How was it?

Note: If you did not *"like"* it, you may have been experiencing some internal resistance. You may have had thoughts like *"This is stupid. Or I don't have time for this. Or I doubt this will work."* Your body may have felt nauseous or uncomfortable. You may have felt emotions ranging from happiness to irritation or sadness. No worries, none of that is you.

Keep practicing. You can practice gratitude thoughts anytime day or night. You may not currently believe you are grateful for anything, and that may be so. But, remember, a belief is just a thought you keep thinking.

Keep practicing gratitude thoughts and you will begin to believe them. Once you believe them you will begin experiencing gratitude as a way of being. You will *"be"* gratitude; you will *"be"* grateful. It's the Law!

The Law of Flow and Resistance

"Let go and Let God."
- Anonymous

"Those who flow as life flows, know they need no other force."
- Lao Tzo

"What we resist, persists."
- Anonymous

Life is always for you. Therefore, **The Law of Flow and Resistance** says that if you follow the path of least resistance, life works well. It also says that if you fight what is, if you resist, life does not work well.

"Go with the flow."

When you flow with the rhythm of life, circumstances line up in a magical, effortless way. This occurs when you have an intention, and then allow the Law to do its thing. That is not to say that you just kick back and do nothing in life; if you *"be"* lazy, you get lazy results! But, you can cease trying to force things. You can stop attempting to manipulate or control circumstances or people.

It is like putting your boat in a fast moving river. You can move easily down stream, or you can attempt to paddle up stream. Which works better?

After my brother Bob died, I knew I needed to move to Spokane, Washington from Oakland, California to be near my parents and remaining siblings. I did not want to make this move. When I left Washington, I swore I'd never move back, and particularly not to Spokane. Never the less that was the guidance I received, and I listened.

I set an intention, to move to Spokane. I repeatedly affirmed God/Spirits' got my back and it will all work out. When I moved, I had no job, no friends, and no place of my own. At first I lived with my sister.

Within a week of arriving in Spokane I had interviewed and was offered a full-time teaching position at Rogers High School, hands down my first choice of all the area schools. Within a few months I had a bevy of friends. By the end of the year I was renting a beautiful house for $300 per month less than I had paid for the studio apartment I had last rented in Oakland. Additionally, I was making more money.

I didn't make any of that happen, I allowed it. I received it. I did not send my good away by insisting that it had to come in a particular way, or from a particular source. I took actions that were obvious like applying for the job I wanted, but then I relaxed and let go.

Going with the flow is choosing, and then allowing. It is like planting a watermelon seed. You can legitimately expect watermelons to be produced, but you don't demand the exact number of leaves or flowers, or melons on the plant. Neither would you expect the plant to grow if you kept digging up the seed to check its progress. You let it develop. You wait and let it grow. You let the laws (God/Spirit) handle it.

Resistance is the opposite of flow. It is fighting and/or hating what is. When you fight what is, you can never win. Really, it's just insane, stupid, right?

The Law doesn't know no.

When you say I want this, and you put your attention on it, the Law draws it to you. When you say I don't want that, the Laws only know you are focusing your attention on it and will also draw that to you.

Nothing comes into your life uninvited. Remember, it is done unto you AS you believe. You invite things into your life with your attention and your belief. Whether you see a particular thing as desirable or not makes no difference to the Law.

The good news is that even the "bad things" can lead to an insight or awareness of a hidden belief. Your increased awareness becomes the access to new choices, and thus a new experience.

The Law of It's All Good

"A bad day for the Ego is a great day for the Soul!"
– Reverend Michael Bernard Beckwith

The Stupid Things I've Done
"Let your sunlight shine on this piece of dung
And dry it out, so I can be used,
For fuel to warm a bathhouse.
Look on the terrible things I've done,
And cause herbs and eglantine to grow out of them.
The sun does this with the ground.
Think what glories God can make
from the fertilizer of sinning!"
– Rumi

The **Law of It's All Good** says that no matter what, everything is working together for your good.

Remember the law of Life. Life is for you, never against you. Thus, in all things there is a gift.

Whenever there is an upset in life, it is ALWAYS an opportunity for your further growth and development.

My greatest growth has always been preceded by dramatic loss or change. I have lived through the death of a many close friends, death of two siblings and a parent, debilitating illness, life threatening accidents and injuries, the sudden loss of a love relationship, as well as making seemingly unforgivable mistakes.

I have experienced dark times, when I was sure all was lost, and that my life was over. In those circumstances I didn't know how to go on. At times I felt such sadness, grief and pain I thought it would end me. And yet *God/Spirit* was right there with me, helping me to see things differently and begin again.

In the crucible of those experiences qualities of compassion, trust, fortitude, and discernment were forged.

Dr. Howard Thurman writes about certain seeds in the forest that can only germinate after a forest fire. Without the heat they could not come to their full potential. It is so with us. The myth of the Phoenix is one of my favorites.

When Nelson Mandela was sentenced and sent to prison on Robben Island he said that his first thought was something like, *"All is lost."* And then, he had another thought. That thought was in the form of a question. The powerful question he asked himself was, *"What if my going to prison is a necessary part of the plan for my country's freedom?"*

What if the dark times in your life, are a necessary part of the plan for your freedom and the delivery of your gifts?

AN EXCEEDINGLY DARK TIME

"Trials are but lessons that you failed to learn presented once again, so where you made a faulty choice before, you now can make a better one, and thus escape all pain that what you chose before has brought you."
– A Course in Miracles

"Greater emergencies and crisis show us how much greater our vital resources are than we had supposed."
– William James

I share my experience so that it may help you see something about yourself. I will tell you about what happened, *"the victim story,"* how I created suffering for myself, and the work I did to emancipate myself from the victim identity and step into my authentic *Radical Self-Love, Child of God Identity.*

I will give you a bit of the background to the experience I went through, so that you might relate. I started this conscious adventure in 1996. I began to do the transformational work. (I will continue to teach you how to do this work in detail later in the book.) Gradually my work, financial, mental, emotional, and spiritual life all began to thrive. At that time my relationships with *God/Spirit*, friends, family and myself had never been richer and more fulfilling. Every area of life continued to transform. I continued to experience awesome and fun miracles as a part of my daily life.

Every area was wonderful, that is, except my romantic relationships. There had been considerable improvement in terms of the quality of the relationships and my experience, but still, no successful long-term relationship. I felt embarrassed by that. *"I'm a great gal now God/Spirit, what's the hold up?"* I just didn't understand.

I'd vacillate from wanting a husband again, to being fiercely opposed to marriage and then to being resigned that it could ever work for me. I had been through so many relationships that were fraught with worry, doubt, fear, and resentment. My history continually demonstrated that there were hidden beliefs that contradicted my desire for a really good, loving, committed relationship.

From the age of nineteen to the age of forty-six I had been in one relationship after another. The longest that I was single during that time period was six months. In my early thirties, my girlfriends and I used to joke that the best way to get *"over"* a man was to get *"under"* another one. It seemed to work, or so I told myself. In truth I was experiencing the same dissatisfying and unsuccessful relationship over and over again with different men.

My romantic history included dating men who were otherwise committed, emotionally unavailable, didn't have time, were financially irresponsible, incompatible, unreliable, untrustworthy, dishonest, much younger or much older than I. Most of the men I dated loved me, but were uninterested in a long-term committed relationship with me, or I with them. In fairness to them, for most of my dating history I was not a prize partner either.

I consistently attracted the opposite of what I said I wanted. As I continued to do this work, transforming my beliefs, and learning to *Radically Love* myself more and more, the quality of my relationships improved, yet I continued to be unsuccessful. Although I didn't see it at the time, I continued to come from the victim identity when it came to relationships.

On the eve of 2014, I went on a four-day silent meditation retreat with the Agape Spiritual Center in Joshua Tree, California. Amongst other insights, I realized that I was meant to write this book. I also saw that if I were ever going to find *"Mr. Right,"* I'd have to stop playing around.

I knew just what that meant. I had been slacking on my prayer and meditation practices. And, for the past year and a half I had been involved in a once every 6 months or so *"friends with benefits"* situation with a much younger man who was my physical trainer. We loved each other, but really, it was never going to be more than that. I let the *"benefits"* part go and kept the friendship.

I ignored the promptings about writing the book, but started practicing *Radical Self-Love* and consciously embracing my authentic *Radical Self-Love, Child of God Identity.* My prayer, meditation, writing, intention setting and affirmation work expanded, and so did I.

I was determined to train my thinking and align with spiritual law and practice the presence of *God/Spirit* and to embody *Radical Self-Love.*

In prayer, I asked to see any false beliefs that blocked me from embodying *Radical Self-Love*. I knew if I could see them, then I could do the work to release them. I got just what I prayed for.

In June of that year I met a man unlike any I had ever dated.

The romance was fast, and intense. We met each other's families and friends within the first month. He was exactly what I had always dreamed of, and nothing like I expected. We were unbelievably compatible, and the same age. We fell in love and began almost immediately to make plans for the future. We agreed that we would *"never grow old together."*

We had an amazingly intimate connection and had such fun together. There was little to no friction in our interactions. The only difficulty was that we lived in cities that were roughly five hours apart. We would see each other on weekends and holidays only.

Nine months later, when he suddenly broke up with me, over the phone, the day before I was to visit him for my spring break I was in shock and intense pain. His explanation was that he was out of integrity in every area of his life, and that he wasn't feeling present to the relationship. I never heard from him again. To this day, I don't know exactly what was going on with him.

What I now know is that it was one of the best things that ever happened to me. I owe that man a debt of gratitude.

I experienced love, joy, playfulness, generosity, tenderness, intimacy and care in that relationship like I had never known. He had become my best friend. I loved and adored him, and I probably would have never left. It was a blessing that he did.

I realized in hindsight that there were behaviors I chose to ignore. He may have loved me, but he was not being honest about his life, and I was lying to myself about it.

After he broke up with me, it seemed like everything I did or saw reminded me of him. I missed him terribly and I was so confused by how it had ended. It was in many ways, the hardest thing I have ever gone through.

As a result of the deep pain of that sudden loss, I immersed myself in this work and crawled up into the heart of *God/Spirit*. I prayed and meditated multiple times a day. I wrote purge after purge, (I'll describe how to do this in Chapter 9.), and talked to my spiritual advisors frequently. I prayed for him and did many of the forgiveness exercises I describe in later chapters. I also reached out to family and friends and received incredibly loving support. My wonderful sisters and their families fed me and cared for me literally and spiritually.

I did not run from, fight with, or deny the pain of that loss. I went through it, and *God/Spirit* was right there with me.

As a result, I had life altering insights about the victim beliefs that had been creating my romantic life. I finally saw those beliefs for the lies they were. I took responsibility for having created all of it. Here is what I saw.

When I was 12 years old my sister Marie committed suicide. She was a gun enthusiast and would make her own bullets.

Two days before she shot herself I helped her make bullets for the gun she used. When I found out that she had used that gun, and those same bullets I knew that it was my fault. I knew that I would have to spend the rest of my life hiding it and trying to make up for it at the same time. When I took the Landmark Forum in 2011 I saw that story, and the subsequent *"It's my fault belief,"* for what it was-a story I made up as a frightened little girl. I was able to drop it and forgive Marie.

What I failed to see was that I had not forgiven myself. My sister was pregnant when she shot herself. The baby died. I believed that I was an unforgivable, baby killer and deserved to be punished. I believed I was a danger to those I loved and didn't deserve a family. I thought and said those things, believed them, and then I created my love life from those beliefs.

Boy oh boy. I also got to see that I had blamed *God/Spirit* for that man's behavior. I had asked *God/Spirit* to block the relationship if it wasn't right, and *God/Spirit* didn't do that. I surmised that *God/Spirit* was punishing me, when in fact, if anyone; I was punishing me.

I had attracted him. He was the perfect man to deliver to me exactly what I believed I deserved- punishment. Actually, he was the answer to my prayer.

Although I had a great relationship with *God/Spirit*, I was still playing the victim. I was mad at *God/Spirit*. No matter how much *God/Spirit* loved me, the Law is. **It is done unto you As you believe.** I got exactly what I believed, and that experience provided the opportunity to see those hidden beliefs. I got to see them clearly for lies that they were.

We are like Captain Picard on the show *Star Trek* who finishes his commands to his crew with the phrase *"Make it so."* I believed and the Law *"Made it* so," over, and over again. *God/Spirit*, via the Law was only giving me what I was asking for. I now know, that I can make a different choice, a better choice.

I got very clear about what the beliefs- I am unforgivable, dangerous, and deserve punishment-had cost me as I described earlier. I accepted it. I accepted what I had done, and took responsibility for the results.

I forgave him and I forgave myself.

The next step was to begin creating a new habit of belief consistent with my *Radical Self-Love, Child of God Identity*. I began using the following affirmations.

I am wholly loveable and wholly loving. I am wholly forgivable, wholly forgiving and forgiven. I am wanted. I am needed. I am loved. I am appreciated. I am valued. I am worthy. I am innocent. I am enough. I deserve the very best of everything. I am safe. I trust in God.

Believe me it takes practice to create a new habit of thought. I touched on affirmations earlier, and I will teach you how to do this kind of training in the next chapter.

Despite the fact that I had taken several workshops on *"soul-mate"* love, which definitely assisted me in loving myself, I had not put what I'd learned into practice when it came to dating. One of the guidelines was to wait at least ninety days before getting physical with a man. I had never even come close to that.

Once I took responsibility and began to affirm the new beliefs I began to see men and dating from a different perspective.

I could finally see that waiting was healthy and *Radically Self-Loving*. I now understand that it is important to know a man over time before taking that very intimate step. It really does take time to get to know whether intellectual, emotional, spiritual and physical compatibility are genuine. Furthermore, it takes time to see if a man is capable of and willing to make a true commitment.

When you know better, you do better. I just didn't know.

As I continue to affirm my new beliefs, I find them easier to remember and say. They are beginning to be activated.

I am so grateful. I feel so loved. I feel the love of *God/Spirit*, and others. I feel the love I have for myself. I feel it in my heart as a peaceful, gentle, calm feeling. All is well.

I have not started dating again yet, but I know that I deserve to be loved, cherished and adored. I deserve to have a loving committed relationship with myself first, and a man second.

It was that dark time that gave me the gift of understanding what I am, where I come from and how this thing really works. I am *Radical Self-Love, a Child of God*. Who I am in any given moment is my choice. I can choose to be Radically Self-Loving and forgiving or a victim who is resentful and unforgiving.

Without that dark time, I would not have seen the hidden beliefs that, up until then, had prevented me from having a successful love relationship. Without that dark time I would not have written this book, nor would I be free to create a life that is totally consistent with my *Radical Self-Love, Child of God Identity*.

I want to end this chapter with a poem by Galaway Kinnell that is both hilarious and spot on. It made me smile and has given me something to shoot for in my romantic life.

Let our scars fall in love...
"We're all seeking that special person who is right for us.
But if you've been through enough relationships you begin to
suspect there is no right person, just different flavors of wrong.
Why is this?
Because you yourself are wrong in someway; and you seek
partners who are wrong in some complementary way.
But it takes a lot of living to grow fully into your own
wrongness.
And it isn't until you finally run up against your deepest demons
your unsolvable problems-the ones that make you who you truly
are-that you are ready to find a lifelong mate.
Only then do you finally know what you're looking for.
You're looking for the wrong person. But not just any wrong
person- the right wrong person-someone you lovingly gaze upon
and think, "This is the problem that I want to have."
Then you will find that special person who is wrong for you in
just the right way."

– Galaway Kinnell

CHAPTER 7 SUMMARY

- Your word is what you say or think, and the promises you make.
- You create your life with your word.
- Spiritual laws, like natural laws are impersonal.
- Ignorance of the Law does not exempt you from the consequences.
- Spiritual laws, like gravity, work regardless of your belief in them or opinion about them.
- A demonstration is the results of your use of Spiritual Law whether it is harmonious or not.
- Demonstrations (effect), come from your actions, and your actions are a direct match with your beliefs (cause).
- The **Law of Life** is that there is infinite good and *God/Spirit* wants to give it to you.
- The **Law of Mind in Action is** It is done unto you, AS you believe.
- The **Law of Karma** is that you get back what you give or put out in the world.
- The **Law of Multiplicity** is that you get back what you put out, amplified, or in an exaggerated fashion.
- The **Law of Focus** is that whatever you focus on in your life grows bigger.
- The **Law of Asking** is that if you ask you will be given, and if you seek will find what you are looking for.
- The **Law of Opposites** provides the perfect environment for you to create what you are asking for. Often the environment appears to be the exact opposite condition of what you are asking for.
- The **Law of Gratitude and Appreciation** says that what you appreciate appreciates- gets bigger.
- The **Law of Flow and Resistance** says that if you follow the path of least resistance, in other words, go with the flow, life works well. The Law also says that if you fight what is, if you resist, life does not work well.
- The Law does not know no. It only knows what you put your attention on.
- The **Law of It's All Good** says that no matter what, everything is working together for your good.
- Upsets, *"Dark Times,"* or seeming mistakes are always an opportunity for growth and development.

Chapter 8
Practicing The Presence and Training Your Thinking

The Only Way you Coast is Down Hill

"A belief is just a thought you keep thinking."
– The Abrahams-Hicks

"It is still up to you to choose to join with truth or with illusion.
But remember that to choose one is to let go of the other."
– A Course in Miracles.

I choose truth. You?

I wish I could tell you that this work was a one and done kind of thing. I kept hoping someone would just sprinkle me with magic fairy dust and poof, I would transform! Nope. Sorry, that's not how it works.

It is however, a fairly simple equation:

New Habit of Thought = New Beliefs =
New Action = New Life Experience

It is very simple, and it takes consistent effort.

The term deep practice has been used to describe the type of practice that is necessary to acquire any skill or talent. Deep Practice causes the brain to produce neuronal circuits that are faster and become automatic. In order to practice deeply you must persist until mastery results. You also must continue to practice to maintain and improve that which you have mastered.

In other words, you have to grapple with something you can't do, continue to flail until you can do it. You must consistently, deliberately continue to do this to become talented or skilled at anything. You must keep practicing or the skill will atrophy. That is how your brain gets habituated- you practice, practice, and practice!

Think of it like you do vitamins. You take one a day. You would not down a month's or a year's worth of vitamins all at once, thinking *"Glad that's taken care of!"* No, you would take them every day. The improvement in your health would develop over time. So it is with your new habits of thought. You must practice daily.

Neurons are the special cells that carry the electrical impulses to different areas of the brain as you think or act. Scientists can measure brain activity by tracing the electrical impulses occurring in neurons and between neighboring neurons.

The rule of thumb in neuro-science is, *"Neurons that fire together wire together. "* This means that neurons that fire in sequence repeatedly develop a pattern of firing. And the more frequently they do this, the faster they fire.

Thus Deep Practice results in the *"re-wiring"* of your brain. Your brain develops more effective pathways when you repeatedly fire the neurons in that new sequence.

Since deep practice works to become talented at playing the piano or hitting a baseball, it will also work for you to become talented at consciously creating your life. You can develop the habits of mind (beliefs) that are consistent with your authentic *Radical Self-Love, Child of God Identity.* You can develop any belief you wish to cultivate.

The only way I know to become a grateful, compassionate, loving person is to deeply practice BEING those ways, when it's not easy- like when someone takes the donut you wanted, or cuts you off in traffic, or is impatient and yells at you. It's deep practice time Baby!

It takes daily, devoted practice to:

1) Know and come from your authentic *Radical Self-Love, Child of God Identity*, and

2) Distinguish when you are coming from the Imposter victim identity, stop it, and return to your authentic *Identity*.

PRACTICE, PRACTICE, PRACTICE

"You must learn to change your mind about your mind."
– A Course in Miracles.

"Be transformed by the renewal of your mind."
– Romans 12:2

Morning and/or Evening Spiritual Practice

If you want to get good at anything you have to consistently, deeply, practice. It takes practice to connect with God/Spirit and *Radically Love Yourself*. It takes practice to believe and know that you are *Radical Self-Love, a Child of God*. It takes practice to stay present in this now moment.

If it were easy, everyone would do it.

Your practice is just like practice for an athlete who is preparing for a game, only *"game-time"* is your life. I practice, so when it's *"game time"* I am more likely to roll with my authentic *Radical Self-Love, Child of God Identity*, rather than the victim identity.

My morning practice includes prayer, gratitude, listening to music, reading and study of sacred text and/or inspirational material, journaling, meditation, setting intentions and a short "coffee" walk. I spend anywhere from thirty minutes to two and a half hours depending on what I am dealing with and what I'm up to.

In the late afternoon I meditate and pray for about twenty minutes.

Just before I go to sleep I do a forgiveness ritual, set intentions for the sleeping hours, and ask powerful questions, all of which takes about five minutes.

Relax. I didn't start out that way. When I first started a spiritual practice it looked like this: My morning began with a cup of coffee and the serenity prayer, maybe a couple minutes of deep breathing and reading a daily reflection book. I would pray through out the day, if I remembered. At night I'd say a quick pray and that was about it.

My practice has grown, obviously. Daily practice is a highly personal and intimate appointment with *God/Spirit*. Each person must find their own path- what works for them. My practice is ever changing, dynamic, and expansive, just like me. You can develop one that works for you.

Prayer

> "Pray without ceasing. In all circumstances give thanks."
> - 1 Thessalonians: 5: 17-18

> "Prayer does not change God, but it changes he who prays."
> – Kierkegaard

The first thing I do before I get out of bed in the morning is pray. I always say the Serenity Prayer, and several others in which I declare the intention that I do *God/Spirits'* will and that I be a vehicle of service for *God/Spirit*.

After my initial prayer I go straight into gratitude and the remaining aspects of my spiritual practice. I always conclude my practice with prayer, and pray and use affirmations frequently throughout the day.

I practice many types of prayer: traditional Christian prayers, Affirmative prayers, and plain old talking to *God/Spirit* about what going on with me prayers.

Some of my short but sweet standard prayers are:

Thank you! I Love you!

Thy will. Or Thy will, not mine.

Use me.

Help. Or Help me.

God/Spirit, please help me to remember to remember what I am and where I come from.

Some of my favorite Christian prayers include the Lord's prayer, the Saint Francis prayer, the Serenity prayer and the Rosary. My favorite Affirmative prayers are included in Ernest Holmes' books *This Thing Called You*, and *This*

Thing Called Life, as well as US Anderson's book *Three Magic Words*, and *Your Needs Met* by Jack Addington and Cornelia Addington.

Gratitude

I use the gratitude practice I gave instructions for earlier. For convenience I will repeat the instructions now.

When you wake up, before you get out of bed practice being grateful. Say out loud at least 5 times each of the following.

1) Thank you for _____. (The names of 5 specific persons or animals.)
2) Thank you for _____. (5 specific other blessings.)
3) Thank you for _____. (5 specific challenges.)
4) Thank you for _____. (5 specific gifts or talents you have.)
5) Thank you! (5 times for nothing at all.)
6) Thank you for this day!

Music

Music is soul food! I like to listen to what I call *"sacred music"* before I continue my practice while I am getting a cup of coffee, making my bed etc. Sometimes I dance and sing, or just listen. It is always up lifting and helps me to center during study and meditation.

Some of my favorite *"sacred music"* artists are Rickie Byars Beckwith, Lecrae, and JR. I also like to listen to classical music, old school Jazz music, nature sound recordings and Tibetan bell music as part of my morning time. I will talk more about the positive effects of music in Chapter 10.

Inspirational Reading

I like to read. I admit it. I have four different daily reflection books that I read in the morning. I also like reading The Bible and other metaphysical books as *God/Spirit* inspires me.

I strongly suggest using a dictionary to look up words, especially if you think you know what they mean. I am constantly surprised and delighted to find out just how little I know. For example, I read that *God/Spirit* was trustworthy.

Trustworthy *means worthy of trust.*

But what does that really mean?

Worthy *means estimable, honorable, meritorious, deserving, fit or safe for.*

Trust *means to place confidence, depend, hope, to commit or place in one's care or keeping; to permit to stay or go or to do something without fear or misgiving, to rely on, or expect confidently.*

Well OK! Thanks! It's nice to know that. Count me in. I love that.

God/Spirit is fit or safe for me to place my confidence in. I can depend and rely upon *God*/Spirit to care for me. Trust in *God/Spirit* means that I can stay or go or do something without fear or misgiving because I can confidently expect that *God/Spirit* has got my back. *God/Spirit* is honorable. That's nice. It's very nice. It's very comforting.

If I start the day with clarity, truth and right thinking, my day goes much better than if I don't. Inspirational reading elevates my focus, so that I am more likely to come from my *Radical Self-Love, Child of God Identity.*

Additional Journaling

I frequently do a bit of journaling before I meditate.

I strongly suggest journaling before meditation, especially if you are experiencing loud and disturbing mind chatter. I have found that if I can get the thoughts out of my head and onto the paper I am less likely to take the disturbing thoughts seriously. I simply *"barf"* them all up and then I am done with them. I give specific instructions for a technique known as a *"purge"* in Chapter 9. It can be a useful tool when you have a big upset.

A great book and guide to daily journaling is Julia Cameron's, *The Artist's Way*. Amongst other things, she teaches a process called the morning pages that I have found to be extremely effective.

I also frequently write after meditation or reading sacred text. Many of the insights and creative ideas that come through me arrive during study, meditation, or while I am running. Occasionally they come in the middle of the night. I either write them in my journal or use the voice dictation application on my phone to record them. I have often found that if I don't write or record them immediately, I can't remember them later.

Meditation

"Be still and know that I am God."
– Psalm 46: 11

"God is Love."
– 1 John 4: 8

"Don't just do something, sit there."
– Anonymous

Why meditate? Based on scientific and anecdotal evidence, meditation is undeniably beneficial and promotes emotional, mental and physical wellness.

Our natural state is to commune with the presence within. Meditation is a time set aside to practice communion. To *"Be still and know."* Know *Radical Self-Love*, experience it for yourself.

There are many types of meditation. I have practiced TM (Transcendental Meditation), used guided meditation tapes, Joppa (sacred sound) meditation, the Hicks Vortex meditations, walking meditations, sacred gong meditation, affirmation meditation, gazing at a candle and focusing on my breath, simply focusing on my breath and many more forms of meditation.

There are excellent guided meditation audio CDs, downloads, phone apps, books, workshops, classes, retreats and teachers who can instruct you in the art of meditation.

The most important aspect of any meditation practice is that it appeals to you enough that you will do it consistently. I meditate first thing in the morning and in the late afternoon. I set aside that time. I rarely miss it, but if I do, I miss it. It is my time to connect, to commune with *God/Spirit* without distractions. I do not judge my meditation time. It is the way I honor myself and make myself available to consciously experience the Presence of *God/Spirit*. It is a way of communing with, being with and knowing *God/Spirit*. It is *Radically Self-Loving* behavior.

I will describe a simple meditation. You can try this and see if it suits you. Try it for 5 minutes or more.

Begin by sitting in a chair comfortably with your feet flat on the floor, your spine straight, and your hands comfortably in your lap.

Take three very deep breaths in and out through the nose. Hold the breath to a count of three at the peak of each inhalation before exhaling.

Then allow your breath to normalize. Invite *God/Spirit* into your awareness.

Focus on the breath. Visualize (imagine) breathing into your heart space. During the inhalation breathe in Peace or Stillness; on the exhalation circulate Love or Beauty to every cell in your body. If it is helpful, imagine a wave of Love flowing into your heart and a wave of Peace flowing out from it.

Finish with three deep breaths, just like at the beginning, and conclude with either a prayer or affirmation and an expression of gratitude for the blessings you have and the blessing that you are. You can say *"Thank you for _____ (mention a person, place or thing). I bless _____ and I bless myself."*

Morning Intentions

"To love and to be loved is to feel the sun from both sides."
– David Viscott

"...Every thought you have brings either peace or war; either love or fear. A neutral result is impossible because a neutral thought is impossible."
– A Course in Miracles

I have found that setting intentions is extremely powerful. It is *Radically Self-Loving.*

Intention *means a determination to act a certain way, resolve, purpose, design, aim, end, objective or goal.*

Before setting intentions I ask the following question -What way of being would *God/Spirit* have me personify today? God/Spirit will always answer any question you ask. I pause and then write down what comes.

Remember you are your word. You create your life with your habitual thoughts, beliefs, words, and actions. Verbalizing your intentions, your purpose, aim, or objective for the day is therefore a powerful tool.

Think of it this way, in order to hit any target you must know what you are aiming at. If you vaguely state that you want to be "more *positive*" or "*act nice,*" you'll get equally vague results. If instead you intend specifically to be "*joyous,*" you give yourself a focused way of being and thus acting for the entire day.

In my journal I write a short letter to *God/Spirit*. I start with saying thank you for the day and then I write three affirmative statements, followed by some short prayers and a final acknowledgement.

The first intention is written as an "I am" statement, the second as a "you are" statement and the third as a "she is" statement. These cover all the ways of relating to yourself. For example:

Dear God/Spirit,

Thank you! Thank you for all the gifts I am aware of and those I am oblivious to receiving.

I Carol am loved, loving, kind and generous.

You Carol are loved, loving, kind and generous.

She Carol is loved, loving, kind and generous.

Thank you so much. I am willing to be guided, guarded and protected. Thy will not mine. Use me. Amen, Ashe, Alleluia, and so it is.

Love Carol

When I set intentions for the day I provide myself with a specific way of being as a focus for my attention, thinking and actions.

So here's a secret: when you begin to embody one quality of *God/Spirit* such as being loving or grateful, all of the other qualities start crashing the party.

Try being grateful and see if loving and peaceful don't sneak into your way of being. Try being joyous and see if light-hearted spontaneous enthusiasm doesn't bust in on the scene.

In other words, these qualities are a package deal! When you embody one quality of *God/Spirit* you can't help expressing a whole host of them.

I always finish my intention letter with two additional intentions: *Thy will not mine and Use me.* Why would I do that?

I used to be afraid to intend this. I use to think that the will of *God/Spirit* was going to be that I suffer and learn painful lessons that would leave me poor, sick and unattractive. If *God/Spirit* used me, wasn't I going to be a door-mat for others?

I was pretty sure it would mean that I'd never have sex again, and probably would have to give up sugar. I didn't trust that *God/Spirits'* will was really for my highest good. I thought it might be a trap.

I was wrong. I now know better.

The law of Life says that there is infinite good and God/Spirit wants to give it to me. God/Spirit has already given me everything I need to express my Radical Self-Love, Child of God self.

However, I must be receptive. I must choose it. God/Spirit can only do for me what it can do through me- use me, work through me.

Hear that again: **God/Spirit can only do for you what it can do through you.** When you pray *"use me,"* you are always asking *God/Spirit* to work through you to express your highest and greatest good. And what blesses one blesses all.

The will *of God/Spirit* is that I express life fully and in the most *Radically Loving* way possible. And that's true for you too. While it is natural for me to express my creative best self, I don't know ahead of time what that looks like in any given moment. Why? Because every moment is new.

What I now know is that I want to be my best. I know that if I am willing, that I am always given what I need, when I need it, for as long as I need it. I also know that when I ask, I am given guidance in a way that I can under-stand.

What is true for me is equally and abundantly true for you.

I want to be the best me I can be. I want to be a channel of goodness, ex-pressing my gifts for others and myself. I want to align my will, with *God/Spir-its*. I know that *God/Spirits'* will is much greater than any trifling plan my ego mind could come up with. I also know that since I have been setting those intentions daily that my life has never been better.

I believe that the best is yet to come for me. The best is yet to come for you too!

I want *God/Spirit* to use me. I want to do the will of *God/Spirit*, not that of my ego mind; so I intend it.

It is a great launching pad for the day!

Coffee Walk

Did I mention I LOVE coffee? Well I do. The final part of my practice is to grab a cup of coffee and head out for a ten minute walk. I use this time to connect with nature and practice gratitude and appreciation.

Nature is lavish and abundant and beautiful! Even if you are in an urban setting, you can connect with it. You can commune with the trees, the grass growing in the sidewalk, the sky, the clouds, the sun, and the wind. It is soul food!

Evening Forgiveness Ritual

> "...Love your enemies, and pray for those who persecute you, that you may be Children of your Heavenly Father."
> – Matthew 5: 44-45

Just before bed I complete the day with my daily general forgiveness ritual. I will discuss more specific work around forgiveness in a later section.

You might ask, *"Why practice daily forgiveness? It sounds horrible!"*

My answer is simple: I like to sleep peacefully. If I am angry, resentful, or upset with another, or myself, I don't sleep well. Those ways of being are inconsistent with my *Radical Self-Love, Child of God Identity.*

Here is my nightly practice. I sit quietly for a moment, take a few breaths and center myself. I ask *God/Spirit* to bring into my mind anyone or anything I am judging, resenting, or in any way have put out of my heart. I ask God/Spirit to help me see the truth and to forgive others and myself.

If I am having difficulty being willing to forgive, I ask *God/Spirit* to do it for me through me. If I don't feel immediate relief, then I do a purge about the person, place, thing or situation in question.

Next, I make a declaration by saying out loud:

"I fully and freely forgive _____ (persons name, place, thing or situation), and myself. I declare that I am free and so is everyone else. I pray that God/Spirit's will be done for them and me."

"God/Spirit bless _____ (persons name, place, thing or situation) and hold us in love while we sleep."

I often combine the forgiveness ritual with EFT (Emotional Freedom Technique). I describe EFT in Chapter 10.

Try it right now. Try it with just one person you might be a little irritated with. Try the forgiveness ritual for them and yourself. Do it even if you don't "feel" like it. Do it especially if you don't "feel" like it.

What was it like? Remember, deep practice is how you get good at anything, even forgiveness.

Your freedom and peace are on the other side of resentment and animosity. In exchange for being "right" and resentful, you can be peaceful and loving.

I'd take that deal any day of the week!

By the way, it's OK if you are unwilling to do this right now. Forgive yourself for being unwilling to forgive. Give yourself a hug and just keep reading. You're doing really well.

Evening Intentions

Just before I go to sleep, I set intentions for my sleeping hours. I do this out loud or in writing. My intentions include: restful and peaceful sleep; healing of any bodily conditions that are out of balance; that I have inspirational dreams; that any conscious or unconscious emotional difficulties are resolved; and that any false beliefs and/or resistance is dissolved.

Evening Questions

Once I have stated my intentions, I ask one or more powerful questions, knowing that *God/Spirit* will answer any question I ask. I strongly suggest that you write these questions in your journal. I have often forgotten the questions I asked and have been astonished by the specific answers I've received during the next day or two. Had I not written the question down I would not have realized that I had asked for and received guidance. This kind of demonstration strengthens faith.

Here are some examples of powerful questions for evening use or throughout the day. Remember, guidance is a principle, a Law. It is always available.

Empowering Questions

Is there anything I am resisting that I need to let go of?

What qualities should I focus on developing?

Is there anything I need to know about _____ (fill in appropriately), and if so, what is it that I need to know?

Is there anything I need to do about _____ (fill in appropriately), and if so, what is it that I need to do?

In what way is this life situation asking me to grow?

What is this life situation meant to teach me? How is it benefiting me?

What can I understand from this situation?

How good can it get?

How can I be even more loving to others and myself?

What would I do in life if I knew I couldn't fail?

How wonderful and loving can I be?

How abundant is the Universe?

How can I demonstrate abundance, love, and gratitude in new ways?

What are *God/Spirits'* thoughts about me?

What is the quality or potential within me that is ready to emerge?

What is the best way for me to facilitate my own growth?

How can I be of service to others or myself today?

What is the next right thing for me to do?

How can I see the good in others more clearly?

What is the best use of this next 5 minutes?

How can I see this situation differently?

How can I see others or myself in a loving way?

Just for contrast let me give you some examples of disempowering questions. Remember, the Law will answer any question you ask.

Disempowering Questions

How could this be happening?

What's the worst thing that could happen?

What's wrong with me?

Why is this happening?

Who is to blame?

Why did they do that?

Why don't they do what I want?

Why are other people so annoying?

Why can't I ever catch a break?

Why do I always self-sabotage?

Why questions generally set you up for a disempowering answer and they generate fear. Since the law will answer any question you ask, be sure to ask powerful questions.

A daily spiritual practice is critical and fairly easy to begin. But remember, what's easy to do is easy not to do. I invite you to design a daily routine that you can immediately begin to practice.

Go on, get some paper and do it right now.

If you need to start with something simple, that's fine. Try beginning with two minutes of meditation morning and evening, accompanied by a prayer of your choice. On the other hand you can use any or all of the suggested practices.

This is your practice to design. Take a few minutes to write down an outline of the spiritual practice you are willing to commit to.

At the bottom of the page, write out the following declaration. "I (*your name*) *promise myself to engage in the following spiritual practice.*"

Now pick the times of day that you will commit to your practice, and put it on your calendar. Remember commitment (promises) and intention are powerful activators. You are worth the time and effort.

You may be saying to yourself, "*I don't want to make a promise, because I might not keep it.*" Fair enough, that's exceedingly normal and completely inconsistent with your authentic self.

If you reflect for a moment, you may be quite startled to notice how many times a day you break promises you've made to yourself. Most of the time you ignore these broken promises, or beat yourself up rather than take responsibility for the broken word. This leaves you feeling diminished because you are your promises. Your promises are the word you give to yourself.

For example, in the past I would make a promise to myself to get adequate rest. I would promise myself that I would be in bed by nine p.m. Nine p.m. would come and go and I would ignore the broken promise and stay up till eleven, and beat myself up for it. I'd eat ice cream, pick at my skin, and call myself names. I would wake up exhausted and do something similar the next night.

You can fail to keep your promises (word) to yourself and still honor your promises (word) by acknowledging the broken (promise) word, acknowledging the impact on you and making a new promise to yourself.

Now days, I make that same promise, *"I will be in bed by nine pm,"* but if I realize I'm not going to keep it, I immediately acknowledge that I am not going to keep my promise, I take responsibility for the impact it may have on me, and make a new promise like *"I will be in bed by nine-thirty pm."*

Making promises to yourself and taking responsibility is consistent with your authentic identity and is *Radically Self-Loving*.

Committing to a daily spiritual practice is *Radically Self-Loving*. I make that promise to myself daily, but I don't always keep it, however I do always honor that promise. You can do the same thing.

Once you have begun, you can expand on your practice. I invite you to ask for guidance as to the most empowering practices for you. Remember, guidance is a principle. You will get an answer if you ask.

TRAINING YOUR THINKING

> *"Nourish it with your daily prayer and meditation and by right thought all day long, not fussily pouncing on every thought, but by knowing in a general way that the Presence of God is with you and refusing to give power to error."*
> – Emmet Fox

OK. You may be thinking, "These practices and affirmations sounds lovely, but what about out there-In the real world?"

When you feel powerfully connected, loving, kind, gracious, unself-conscious and fulfilled you are being your authentic *Radical Self-Love, Child of God Self*. No problem-Life is sweet!

But what about when you can't seem to do that? What can you do when you are fussy?

When you are not experiencing yourself as joyous and free it feels off because it is inauthentic. It is inconsistent with your true identity. When that happens, you are likely coming from the victim identity. If it has been your default identity, it will take your intention and attention to come from your authentic *Radical Self-Love, Child of God Identity*.

Just like you would train a dog to behave in ways that are pleasing to you, you can train yourself to come from your authentic *Radical Self-Love, Child of God Identity*.

There are two kinds of situations that call for training:

1) Upsets that pass.
2) Upsets that last.

Upsets that Pass

> "The Storm had rolled away to faintness like a
> wagon crossing a bridge."
> – Eudora Welty

> "We are never upset for the reason we think we are."
> – A Course in Miracles

Lets say you are walking your dog through the woods, and you come upon another dog. Both dogs start barking and growling. Hackles are raised, fangs are bared and hearts are pounding. No worries. They're just being dogs. You and the other owner exchange knowing looks, a wave, and a smile and you are on your way. Your dog may bark a few more times, but she shakes it off and is soon on to the next vista.

Bravo!

This is just like experiencing an emotional upset that comes, is felt, and passes.

At other times, it takes work to let go, and let it pass. I've heard it said that anger past 30 seconds is ego- you're ego is telling and believing a fearful, angry story. You have stepped into the victim identity.

When emotions are allowed to flow, you feel them without attaching any story to them. They come, are felt and then they go. In those instances, you are like the dog that barks madly, shakes it off and moves on.

When an upset persists, it is almost always because you have created a story around the event. Often, an event or thought has triggered a hidden remembrance of a past emotion that, for whatever reason, did not flow.

Emotions are indicators. There is nearly always something about the situation that has brought to the surface an unexamined, un-felt, past emotion.

When you allow yourself to feel the emotion, it can pass, and you stay current. When you experience upsets that persist, it is an opportunity to access a hidden false belief.

Every upset, large or small, can be used to see the false beliefs and victim stories that are creating suffering for what they are- lies.

See and be free.

Upsets that Last

If the upset is out of proportion to the event that *"caused"* it, or if it persists beyond a minute or two, you are likely stuck in a past emotion that was not allowed to flow.

The other possibility is that some type of genuine loss may be occurring that is causing pain.

How can you tell?

A current loss would include a death, illness, injury, accident or the loss of a job, housing, or a relationship etc. In other words, some event is actually occurring in the present. Regardless of the cause, this process can be helpful in moving through any upset, but especially one coming from past trauma.

When something occurs, either in reality, or in your mind, and you find yourself upset, the first thing to do is simply allow yourself to feel it. Or as Reverend Maggie would say, *"If you can feel it, you can heal it."*

When I am upset I ask myself the question, *"How do I feel?"* Not an intellectual exercise, but literally where do I feel it in my body? I breathe and let it pass. If it passes quickly, great, if not, then I engage in further work.

If the upset persists, then I ask a different question and pray. The question I ask is:

"What am I thinking and believing right now that isn't true?"

and I pray,

"Please God/Spirit help me to see the truth about this situation and myself."

In other words, what am I making it mean about me... because when I'm feeling bad; it's always about me. I am telling a story that is making me feel bad. Once again I've forgotten what I am and where I come from. I have forgotten that I am the one creating how I experience my life.

If answering the question and praying gives me an insight that brings me back to a sense of peace, then it's over and I can carry on powerfully. If not, it's time to employ some training, and/or further work.

I love dogs. A good dog trainer has the ability to direct their animal with very simple commands. We can do that too. I use the following commands as a means of training myself to return to my *Radical Self-Love, Child of God Identity* and drop the victim identity.

The commands are:

- **Drop it!**
- **Leave it!**
- **Come!**
- **Stay!**
- **Fetch!**

Drop it!

When you go on a walk with your dog and you notice it has found some poop, or a dead squirrel or a porcupine or the like, and it latches onto it, you use the command- *"Drop it."*

Leave it!

Once the dog has dropped it, he is likely to gaze fondly at the thing and latch back on unless you give a second command- *"Leave it!"*

Come!

And then immediately you issue the command- *"Come!"* Soon the dog is back at your side, safe and mostly unscathed.

Stay!

You then give the final command to assure your dog does not go back to the objectionable thing. You say- *"Stay!"*

Fetch!

Now here's the critical part. Give the dog something else to do! Give him something else to occupy his attention so that he forgets all about the thing and how much he wants it. Here boy *"Fetch!"* And you throw the ball or the Frisbee and your doggie is happy as a clam again.

YOU HAVE DOMINION

> *"Straight thinking may not be the easiest thing in the world, but it is possible for anyone."*
> – Ernest Holmes

I recently had the good fortune to help dog sit a Great Dane named Chloe. She is by nature a sweet, docile and loving animal. She will also, by her dog nature, attempt to dominate anyone who does not show her that they have dominion over her.

She will obey commands when you have asserted yourself and been disciplined in demanding that she obeys your commands. If you do not do this, she will do whatever she pleases. She will not obey you; she will in fact dominate you.

Your thinking is like that. Either you exert dominion over it, or it will dominate you.

I'm going to say that again in a little different way because it is really important.

Just like you do with your dog, **you must exert dominion over your attention** and **your will**.

Dominion *is supreme authority, sovereignty, domain or absolute ownership.*

Attention *means the act or state of applying or directing the mind to something; the act or faculty of attending, especially by directing the mind to an object.*

Will *means deliberate choice, willingness, consent, intention, volition or determination.*

No one else can do this for you.

Did you hear what I said?

No one else has supreme authority over how you choose to direct your mind.

Not even *God/Spirit.*

You have to make the deliberate choice to discipline your thinking. If you do, then *God/Spirit* can help you see things differently.

I was taught that you may not be able to control the first thought that comes to mind, but you are responsible for the second and the third and so on. What you focus on grows. Through the Law, your attention magnetizes more of the same.

Have you ever noticed that when you entertain thoughts of self-pity that it doesn't take long before you are dredging up all kinds of memories of old hurts or perceived slights? The momentum builds until it seems to have a life of its own.

I can remember one afternoon driving down the 580 freeway on my way to class at Cal State Hayward. A song came on the radio that reminded me of an old boyfriend, and I started wandering down a victim identity *"He done me wrong!"* kind of path. Before I knew it I was ready to pull off the freeway, park my truck and just forget everything. I thought I ought to just walk into the hills never to be seen again.

Instead, I caught myself. I ask the question, *"What am I thinking and believing right now that isn't true?"* and I prayed, *"Please God help me to see the truth about myself and this situation."* I realized that I was telling myself a story that since that relationship hadn't worked that my life was pointless and worthless, and that I was also pointless and worthless. That drop of sewage victim identity story was just a story- It wasn't true.

I dropped it. I left it. I didn't fight with it, or make it wrong, or deny that the thought was there, or believe it. I let it alone. I used dominion over my attention to come away from the story. I stayed with myself and I commanded my attention to fetch the truth-affirmations.

I started affirming. I said out loud several affirmations *"I am never alone. I am loved. All is well. I am divinely supported. I am enough."*

The next thing I knew, I said to myself something like *"How about if we just go to class, and then go home."* So that's what I did- crisis averted. Fifteen minutes later I was laughing with my friend about it-ridiculous, and very funny.

Let's look at these commands a little more closely.

Drop it!

Drop *means to cease to be concerned, to let fall, to set down, unload, to give up as an idea, to break off an association or connection with.*

Dang! That's deep!

In order to drop it, you must see that you've grasped that juicy turd of a victim identity story.

Typically, in life, something happens, and you say something to yourself about it. If what you say makes you feel good or produced a neutral emotion, no problem. But, if it upsets you, it's a red flag.

If you can see the story you are telling yourself, drop it. It's just a story. Maggie would say, *"It's like a sticky fork."* If you sat down to have some pancakes or waffles and your fork somehow got into the syrup, you would go wash it off, so you could enjoy your breakfast. It's uncomfortable to eat with a sticky fork. It's no big deal. You'd just wash it. You wouldn't beat yourself up because your fork got in the syrup; you'd simply wash your fork.

When I notice I'm telling a victim story I will say *"Oops! That makes me sticky."* Or I'll say *"Oops! I'm telling a victim story! There's a better choice."* Saying these things helps me drop the story in a neutral kind of way. I don't have to beat myself up because I have a sticky fork. I don't have to beat myself up for telling a victim story. I just need to drop it. The same goes for you.

Another simple example of being neutral when you make a *"mistake"* is when you notice that you are speeding. I was coming back from Priest Lake the other day. The speed limit on highway 57 is 60 miles per hour. I'm trundling along listening to a Rickie BB album and all of the sudden I realize I'm going 75 miles per hour! *"Oops!"* I say to myself, *"Pump your brakes Carol."* No big deal, I just slowed down.

Pump your breaks. Wash your fork. It ain't no thang.

Leave it!

To **leave** *is to fail to include or take along with, to go away from, to depart or terminate association with.*

Perfect, just what the doctor ordered.

Once the story has been distinguished, leave it alone. This is the point at which you must exert your will- turn your attention to something else. I always ask *God/Spirit* to help me with this.

Come!

Come *means to move towards something; to move or journey to a vicinity with a specified purpose, to reach a condition.*

Come back to what you are and where you come from. You are not your victim identity story; you are not your emotions, your thoughts, your body sensations. You are *Radical Self-Love, a Child of God.*

This is where affirmation is critical. Affirm the core beliefs that are consistent with your authentic *Radical Self-Love, Child of God Identity.*

However, if you are not convinced that your victim identity story is just a story, and you are pretending to your self that it is true, you are back in the victim identity.

Affirming from the victim identity is like putting hot fudge and whip cream on a turd and calling it an ice cream Sunday-it doesn't work. It still stinks. You may need to do some more intensive work to drop and leave it. I will address additional work in Chapter 9.

Stay!

To **stay** *is the action of halting; to fix on something as a foundation.*

Your foundation is your authentic *Radical Self-Love, Child of God Identity*. To stay with that you must practice it-habitually.

Remember, if you do not replace the habit of being a victim, with the habit of being *Radical Self-Love, a Child of God*, you will revert back to being a victim automatically.

Habit- it is why daily spiritual practice and training is so important.

When I need to "stay" myself, I will often do a mini-meditation by simply closing my eyes and taking a deep breath, holding it and sighing. I simultaneously focus on my heart and ask *God/Spirit* to help me center.

Fetch!

Fetch *means to get and bring something, to realize, to cause to come, to bring about, to bring forth, to take in, to draw.*

Fetching is the perfect chore to give to the ego, or surface mind. It is designed to protect you and accomplish tasks. Since those are the ego's main functions, why not have it do things you want?

You can direct it with questions like:

- What ten things do I have to be grateful for right now?
- What qualities are growing in me right now?
- What things have I learned recently?
- How could I take really good care of myself right now?
- What action would be consistent with *Radical Self-Love*, right now?
- How could I see this differently that would make me laugh or feel good?
- Who could I call to ask how they're doing right now?
- What is the next right thing for me to do?
- How can I see this differently?
- How could I bring peace, light heartedness or joy to this situation right now?"

No Barking!

"Hey!" You might be saying, *"That wasn't on the original commands list!"*

I know, but it is important.

To **bark** *is to advertise by persistent outcry, to speak in a curt, loud and usually angry tone.*

Isn't that just what you do with your victim-identity sewage stories? You persistently advertise how *"They've done it to me again."* in a curt, loud and angry tone. My goodness, such drama!

Once you've dropped a particular story, it's important, to really leave it. Don't start talking about it again- even if it's a REALLY GOOD STORY. It serves no good purpose. It is usually an attempt to garner sympathy or prove that you are right about something or someone. It is victim identity behavior all the way.

Sticky fork alert! You're speedin partner!

CHAPTER 8 SUMMARY

- New Habit of Thought = New Beliefs = New Action = New Life.
- Deep practice is the term used to describe the type of practice that is necessary to acquire any skill or talent.
- You can develop the habits of mind (beliefs) that are consistent with your authentic *Radical Self-Love, Child of God Identity*, through deep practice.
- It takes practice to connect with God/Spirit and *Radically Love Yourself.*
- Morning and evening practices can include: prayer, gratitude, music, inspirational reading, journaling, meditation, intention setting, coffee walks, forgiveness rituals, and asking questions.
- In order to habitually come from your authentic *Radical Self-Love, Child of God Identity* you must discipline your thinking. You must train yourself.
- Emotions are indicators. When emotions are allowed to flow, you feel them without attaching any story to them.
- An upset that passes results when emotions are allowed to flow.

- An upset that lasts results when current events trigger a memory of a past emotion that did not flow.
- An upset that lasts is an indicator that you may have created a story about the event and dropped into the victim identity.
- When an upset persists ask yourself *"What am I thinking and believing right now that isn't true?"* And pray, *"Please God/Spirit help me to see the truth about this situation and myself."*
- You must see the victim identity story as a *"story"* and not the *"truth."*
- You must exert dominion over your attention.
- You can train your mind using the dog training commands.
- The mind training commands are: Drop it! Leave it! Come! Stay! Fetch!
- *"No barking"* is the final command. Do no revisit a story no matter how attractive it may be.

Chapter 9
I'm not buying a Fucking Teddy Bear! – When Upsets Won't Budge

"Humph!" I grunted. "I'm not buying a fucking Teddy Bear! What will people think?"

Maggie laughed, which annoyed me further. *"Oh, lighten up. It doesn't have to be a Teddy Bear, and you can tell anyone who asks that it's for your little girl, and it is."*

"My God it's come to this," I thought as I walked down the toy aisle in the Super K-mart. And there was Ted, sitting amongst the GI-Joe commando toys, a lavender colored, medium sized stuffed gorilla. He was sporting nothing but a smile; and a thin red cord was tied around his neck, the ends of which were tiny heart-shaped pillows.

It was love at first sight. I snatched him off the shelf and briefly held him to my heart, the *"hug-ability"* test, just like Maggie told me to do. It felt real nice, and thank God no one had seen.

Inner Child Work

That was the beginning of my adventures with Ted, and my *"Little Carol."* Yes, indeed-inner child work. I am pleased to report that we've been together happily since 1999.

I was told to find a photograph of myself before the age of five and put it somewhere I could see it frequently. I did that, and began to do mirror work- looking into my own eyes and saying nice things to myself. (I'll talk more about that later.)

As you grow up, traumatic things can happen. In those moments, of stress and fear, as a child you often don't understand and you don't know what to do.

If you didn't have anyone helping you, you likely *"checked-out."* You stopped feeling, and coped with the trauma whatever way you could.

Until and unless those unresolved emotional traumas are addressed, they continue to surface. The child is attempting to get resolution-hence the pre- viously mentioned upsets. *"You are never upset for the reason you think you are."* It is coming from your child-self.

Your personality is multi-faceted, just like everyone else. People speak of having *"different sides"* to their personalities. They are the different roles that the surface mind/ego assign to you. It thinks it is these roles. None of these facets is your authentic *Radical Self-Love, Child of God Identity.*

Let me explain further. Have you ever noticed that you have several differ- ent voices in your head? I've heard it called "the committee," or the IBSC (Itty Bitty Shitty Committee.) My committee consists of the following: The Critic, The Bitch, The Whiner, The CEO, The Slut, The Prude, The Worm, The Sweetie, The Smartie Pants, The Rebel, The Smart-Ass, The Clown, The Skep- tic, The Wise One, and *Little Carol.*

As a young adult I wanted desperately to be a *"good"* person, and I knew I wasn't. So, instead I sought to be the best at being *"bad."* The drinking, and wildly self-destructive behavior that accompanies that life style, nearly killed me.

I was sure that being all of me was unacceptable. I judged and really hated parts of my personality. I wanted to get rid of the parts that I deemed unac- ceptable- the parts of me that I blamed for acting in ways that I felt were shameful, or caused me to feel guilt or doubt, the parts of me that had made poor choices, and so called mistakes. I either wanted get rid of them, or hide them really well.

The committee had been ignoring *"Little Carol"* for a very long time, or worse, yelling at her, telling her to shut up. It seems she didn't have a voice or a vote. I had spent years abusing and neglecting that part of my personality.

As an adult, you have likely tried to separate from your child-self because you believe it is the source of the pain you experience. You blame that part of yourself. I've heard it said that blame stands for *believing lies and making excuses.* Sounds about right.

I know what that's like-blaming the child-self; it's frightening, lonely and depressing. Today I don't live that way. I find my personality rather amusing and entertaining. I love all of me, including my at times unruly personality facets.

At first, this all sounded crazy to me, but I had to admit, it felt good to hold Ted or look in the mirror and say *"I love you honey."* I would look at the picture of my young self, and lovingly talk to her like I would one of my nieces. It took a long time before I could do any of this without weeping.

I have participated in Inner Child workshops, and used several books designed for just this kind of work. Inner Child work can be powerful for anyone, but especially for those who have suffered childhood trauma.

I had to learn how to dialogue with *"Little Carol."* I use my journal to communicate with her. I asked her lots of questions. What do you want me to know? What do you need? Tell me what that was like for you? What do you need to say? What do you need to hear?

I learned how to tell her I love her, and that I will always take care of her. I learned to tell her that I'm proud of her, and that she is doing a great job. I learned how to encourage her, and take care of her. I learned to treat her with respect, kindness, consideration and love.

I would journal these dialogues and hold Ted. I learned that it was important to find healthy ways to soothe her. I learned how to comfort her when she was afraid or sad, or angry. I will teach you how to do this in Chapter 10. It has taken a long time for her to trust me, and I continue to do the exercises and practices described in Chapter 10.

Darned if it doesn't work. I can honestly say I love my *"Little Carol"* and all of the other aspects of my personality. This kind of work is transformational. I have learned to accept, love and care for all aspects of my personality, without mistaking any of them for my real Self. I think of if this way, they all get a seat at the table. They can sit down, have a cup of tea or cocoa, but they're not in charge.

When I experience an upset that persists, the upset is most likely coming from "*Little Carol*" and it's time to do some work with Ted. A little later on I will explain how to do an exercise called purging that is a great tool to get resolution of emotional upsets that persist.

None of this training came easily for me. My intention is that the guidance I offer will make your inner work journey at least smoother. While it will require effort on your part I can help you eliminate many of the errors that I made.

Now it's Your Turn

Use the following tools to work specifically with your child-self or "inner child."

1) Frame a photograph of yourself when you were no more than five years old and place it somewhere you will see it frequently. At least twice a day look at the photograph and call your child-self by name and say "I love you."

2) Buy a stuffed animal, or at least a nice soft pillow that feels good when you hug it. Make sure you test it with the "hugability" test before you buy it. You will use it to hold and hug when you are dialoging with your child-self. The "hugability" test is done as follows: wrap your arms completely around the stuffed animal and hold it to your heart while you take a deep breath. If it feels good and/or relaxing then it has passed the test.

3) Use your journal to begin a dialogue with your child-self while holding your stuffed animal or pillow. Imagine you are holding your child-self. You will use your journal to write to your child-self, and give it the opportunity to respond to you. Start by apologizing for ignoring, yelling at, or mistreating your child-self. Explain to your child-self that you now understand that it is your job to love and take care of it. Tell your child-self that you didn't know any better and that you are now learning how to take care of it. Say whatever you wish to comfort and acknowledge your child-self such as: You've been so brave and strong; You've done

such a great job; I'm so proud of you; I love you and I will always be here for you. This may feel uncomfortable at first. You child-self probably will not trust you right away, but I encourage you to be persistent.

4) Write out questions directed to your child-self and then write the responses your child-self gives. Ask your child-self questions such as: What do you want me to know? What do you need? Tell me what that (any situation that is or was upsetting) was like for you? What do you need to say? What do you need to hear from me or others? What do need me to do? Respond in writing to your child-self in a loving and compassionate manner. Reassure and soothe your child-self and tell your child-self that you will always take care of it. You may also verbalize these responses in a soothing manner.

5) Most upsets that last are coming from the child-self. Use purging, venting, forgiveness and amends to deal with upsets. (These tools are discussed in the next section.)

6) Use the Radically Self-Loving practices described in Chapter 10 to nurture your child-self.

You can do this work.

Believe me, if I can, so can you. It is never too late to have a happy childhood! This is your opportunity to re-parent yourself. You can heal your mind and thus transform your life. You are *Radical Self-Love, a Child of God*. It is your destiny to know yourself.

PURGING

> "When a situation remains unconscious it shows up as fate."
> – Carl Jung

> "The problem is that you've been looking for love and acceptance
> on a planet with people who don't love and accept themselves.
> And because they don't see you, you use that to invalidate you."
> – Panache Desai

That is the victims' fate.

If I am unable to let loose of a story I do a purge. This is distinct from merely complaining. The intent of a purge is to get the *"poison"* up and out, rather than focusing on the victim-identity story. A purge can help you see that the victim-identity story is not *"the truth,"* so that you can drop it. Purges can also unearth hidden beliefs that are inauthentic. Handwrite this. Do not use a computer unless you cannot write.

Steps for a Purge

The first thing to do is to pray for guidance. Ask for assistance in being honest, and to be given insight and clarity.

Next, write a letter to *God/Spirit* about the situation that includes the following.

Write about the story including everything you are feeling.

Let the person, persons, or institution really have it. Call them every name in the book and tell them about themselves.

Tell them everything that you need to say, why you are angry, resentful, bitter, hurt, sad, frustrated, etc. Get it all on paper.

Tell yourself, including your child-self, anything you need to say to yourself.

Write about what you would rather have done or said instead.

Next write about what it is costing you to hold onto this, in terms of love, freedom, joy, creativity, physical well being etc.

Finally write about what you get out of holding onto this? Do you get to: Be right? Play a victim? Avoid responsibility? Punish others or yourself?

Once you are done, write about what was learned, or what you got out of the experience. What false belief was at play? What insights did you receive?

It may take several sittings to complete this thoroughly. I was in the middle of a huge purge about a relationship break up, I wasn't done, but I needed to stop writing. At that time I lived alone, but I was terrified someone would read this awful stuff I was spewing out.

Maggie suggested that I take my purge notebook put it on a hanger in my closet and put a sweater over it to hide it. That worked for me. I know it sounds ridiculous, but I needed that reassurance. You may need to do something similar if the purge is a big one.

Once the letter is complete write *"thank you"*, and I move on to the next step.

Next, while listening to some loud high-energy music, read the letter out loud with lots of oomph! If you don't have somewhere private to do this you can drive to an isolated spot and do this in your car, or hike to an isolated spot and do it there. I hug Ted, and often cry when doing this step, so I always have tissue handy.

Once you've read it aloud burn it, and give it to *God/Spirit* with a prayer. I say something like:

"OK God/Spirit, take this, and give me back whatever you would like me to have about this. Help me see the truth about myself, and this situation. Help me to remember to remember what I am and where I come from. Thank you! Amen."

You may need to talk to a trusted advisor about the insights you received from doing the purge. Again, if you don't have someone like that yet, that's fine. This process is beneficial nonetheless.

The next step is to do some type of forgiveness ritual, which I will discuss following the section on venting.

VENTING

Venting serves the same purpose as a purge only it is done with a trusted advisor or friend. Instead of writing, you talk the poisonous story out. Again the intention is to get the poison up and out so that you can see it for what it really is.

The caveats I have about venting are: it can lead to dependence upon another person rather than on God/Spirit; and it is easy to slip into merely complaining.

Most often I write first and then talk with an advisor if I am still unsettled about a matter.

Venting is not a substitute for writing.

I use venting sparingly because I have never been particularly skillful at venting without sliding into complaining. When I complain I step firmly into the victim identity and it ends up taking much longer to see what's really going on.

Steps for a Venting

Declare that you merely need to vent. State that the intention is to get the sewage-victim story out so that you can see what's really going on with you. If you tell them your intention, then the person listening can listen with purpose.

Pray either together, or silently that you be given insight and clarity. Ask to see any false belief that is at play.

Use the same steps as the purge only talk rather than write.

I see venting as a way of blowing off some steam so I can get it out of my system. If you've ever been around geese they do this rather nicely. If a pair of geese get into it with one another, they honk at each other loudly, flap their wings furiously and then it's over. They go back to picking at the grass, or whatever they were doing.

Sometimes I just need to honk and flap my wings a little to get back to my peaceful authentic *Radical Self-Love, Child of God Self.*

FORGIVENESS

"I say to you, not seven times [must you forgive your brother]
but seventy-seven times."
– Matthew 18:22

"Holding a resentment is like taking poison and wanting the
other fellow to die.
– Emmet Fox

"If you want to see the brave, look at those who can forgive. If
you want to see the heroic, look at those who can love
in return for hate.
– Hindu Book of Prayers

To **forgive** *means to cease to feel resentment against, to excuse or pardon.*

And **pardon** *means the excusing of an offense without exacting a penalty or to allow to pass, without punishment.*

When someone does something and you resent it, you have created suffering for yourself.

You have either failed to accept what is happening; or you have failed to take a doable action and then blamed the other for it.

You may wish to see the other punished, or want them to apologize, or to do something to make it *"right"* for you.

You want them to *"pay."*

But really who is paying for the resentment? Who is really being punished or penalized?

Forgiving someone does not mean that you have to approve of their behavior or even like them. You don't. However, it is a necessary pre-requisite to self-forgiveness.

What you judge and resent about others is a reflection of your negative opinion of yourself- It is your self-judgments.

When you judge yourself, you project that on others. If you were not judging yourself, you may notice their behavior, but you would not take it personally. You would not resent it. There is an old saying that is rather relevant, *"If you spot it, you've got it."*

I once had a colleague that seemed to me to be extremely intolerant and judgmental. I would complain and complain about this woman and about how narrow-minded she was. I resented it. I resented her.

After a long vitriolic purge about her, I saw that I was the one who was being judgmental, intolerant and close-minded.

Oh my! I also saw that she wasn't an isolated case. Across the board, I was being intolerant of people who were intolerant. I was being judgmental of people who were judgmental. I was being close-minded about people who were close-minded.

It was an opportunity to forgive all of them and myself. I got the chance to choose differently- to begin again.

Until you forgive the so called other person, you will not, cannot forgive yourself. You are not just seeking to forgive the other person; you are, every single time, seeking to forgive yourself.

Stop for a minute and let that in. Take a breath.

You may be thinking *"No, no, NO! They really are being jerks and I'm not!"* Cool it there turbo! You may be right.

Try using the following questions when viewing the behavior of others that seem to disturb you, *"Do I act like that? Or have I acted like that in the past?"* It could be that you are witnessing behavior that you used to engage in, and for which you have not forgiven yourself.

The people, or situations that you resent give you the opportunity to become aware of something that was previously hidden. If you can lean into this, run towards it rather than away, your freedom is on the other side.

Refusing to forgive is like walking around life with clenched fists. You can neither give, nor receive anything when your fists are clenched and it is exhausting! It feels like that when you are unforgiving.

Try this exercise to slam the point home.

Right now set a timer for a minute. Now clench both of your fists as hard as you can for a whole minute straight. If you can't do that tighten some other muscles instead.

What was that like? Imagine living like that! You do the mental, emotional and spiritual equivalent when you refuse to forgive.

Forgiving something does not mean condoning or liking something that you don't. Forgiving means you intend to be *Radically Self-Loving* and free, no matter what.

Resentment is self-abuse. Forgiveness is Radical Self-Love. It is freedom from bondage. When you let others *"off the hook,"* you do the same for yourself.

I recommend the general evening forgiveness ritual and an on-going forgiveness practice that I will cover later. When resentment is persistent in nature, I suggest you purge and then do the following ritual.

Forgiveness Steps for Stubborn Resentments or Hurts

1) Purge the situation completely as instructed above.
2) Allow yourself to feel the dominant emotion generated by the resentment. Ask *God/Spirit* to help you understand anything about the situation or any past situations that would be beneficial.
3) Ask *God/Spirit* to help you to stop taking the situation personally. Ask *God/Spirit* to help you to see the situation from the other person's perspective. Alternately you can ask *God/Spirit* to help you to see that what they did made sense to them.

It is at this point that you may experience compassion for yourself and the other person. Ask *God/Spirit* to help you understand and know that everyone, including yourself, does the best they can at all times.

If it is a very big resentment, you may have to purge the situation many times before you feel peaceful enough to move onto step #4.

4) Next make a declaration of forgiveness. Say something like: "*I fully and freely forgive myself, the other person, and the entire situation. I declare that I am free and so are they. It is over. It is finished.*" Tell *God/Spirit* thanks, and bless everyone involved.

5) From then on, if the person or situation comes to mind, say a quick prayer for the person, and ask *God/Spirit* to help you turn your attention to other matters. My favorite prayer in this situation is simply "*Thy will for (fill in the name), I bless them and release them to your care.*"

It works. In this way you can let go of know-it-all-ism, and trust that there is more going on in any given situation than meets the eye. You can practice trusting and affirming that everything, indeed is working together for the good of all.

CLEAN-UP

Once you have done a purge and forgiveness ritual, you are in a much better position to see if there is anything further action you need to take. If you have behaved selfishly, you may need to clean that up with the person or persons in question. In some circles, this is called making amends.

Amend *means to put right, to change or modify for the better, to improve, to reform oneself.*

Amends are generally advised if your behavior has been unloving, inconsiderate, unkind, overtly dishonest or inauthentic, which is also a form of dishonesty.

Depending on the situation, you can do this directly with the person or indirectly, by simply changing your behavior in the future. Each situation is different. I strongly suggest that you first pray for guidance and then check with one of your advisors before approaching someone directly. If you do not have an advisor yet, use your evening question to ask for guidance on the matter. I suggest you wait at least a week before proceeding with the amends to make sure you are settled about the guidance. I have found it is better to wait if I am unsure. Refrain from making direct amends if to do so may cause any other person further discomfort or harm.

In general, when making a direct amends, acknowledge the harmful behavior and take responsibility for the impact the behavior had on the other person. Apologize and ask if there is anything that you can do to make it right with them. Acknowledge that they are important to you, if appropriate, and tell them your intention for your future behavior.

Indirect or living amends begin the minute you take responsibility for your behavior. It really means to live differently from that moment on.

The greatest living amends you can make is to consistently do the work that empowers you to come from your authentic *Radical Self-Love, Child of God Identity*. When you do this you will naturally treat others with loving kindness and respect, anything less would be inauthentic.

To forgive and make any appropriate amends allows you to walk around free and loving. It empowers you to be the person you were born to be. You get to walk in the world as *Radical Self-Love, a Child of God*.

RESISTANCE

When you begin doing this work, it may seem at first that you going crazy. It may seem that things are actually worse rather than better.

You may think it isn't working and that you were better off before you started this adventure.

What that really means is that your ego, that just loves to play the victim, is resisting your transformation.

That is actually a good sign. It means that you are waking up. You are becoming aware of the inauthentic beliefs that have been running you. These false beliefs are coming up to be released.

Mental chatter may seem to get worse or get louder than before.

You are not getting worse, but simply becoming aware of your habitual thoughts. You are becoming aware of something that has likely been there for much of your life, but was heretofore hidden.

When you become aware of negative mental chatter I suggest you say to yourself something like, *"Thank you for bringing to my attention what I need to release."*

I also suggest praying, practicing self-forgiveness and using the gratitude practice mentioned earlier. These practices along with the *"dog commands"* can be used to restore balance when you are feeling unsteady.

I don't wanna!

You may find yourself at times arguing for your smallness, your limitations, the reasons you can't do this work or be a better person, blah, blah, blah. The reasons may seem plausible, and even realistic.

That's part of the ego resistance. They are really just drops of sewage victim-identity stories.

It's normal to give in to the kind of thinking that has you play it safe one more time. You probably have a habit of playing it safe if you have been coming from the victim identity. It's normal to *"Be reasonable."*

Here's what they may sound like: *"I don't feel like it! It's too hard. It takes too much time and I'm so busy! I'm bored with this! How come other people aren't doing this work? I don't deserve anything better than what I've already got. Why do I have to be responsible? It's too late for me! I just need a little break from all of this spiritual crap! It doesn't feel good so it must not be working! See, I told you this wouldn't work for me, I'm angry, sad, lonely, and/or depressed again! I'm just going to gossip a little."*

Here's what it may look like: You sit down to do your meditation and all of the sudden you just HAVE to clean the toilet. You are in the middle of a purge or sitting through some uncomfortable emotion and all of the sudden you just HAVE to have a hamburger or some ice cream or a drink. You want to get to your prayer and meditation, but you just HAVE to do three more chores, and oh gosh, where'd the time go. You meant to do your affirmations, but you just HAD to find out what whosie-whatsit posted on Facebook.

Resistance may also show up as fatigue, generalized discouragement, anger or frustration. You may be seized by a sense of insecurity, or may find yourself being excessively judgmental or critical. Most often this is a signal that you have temporarily forgotten the purpose of your practice.

We use these kinds of distractions, and various forms of anesthesia to avoid the discomfort of the work. No worries. The pain of resistance and coming from a victim identity will eventually drive you back to doing what will bring you freedom, and peace.

As best you can, don't take it personally when you find yourself engaging in victim-identity resistant behaviors. Do your best to be gentle and loving with yourself.

When I notice I am engaging in resistance I give myself a hug and say something like, *"Oh honey, I love you! You're so silly! We don't go there anymore. What do you need?"* I also use the on-going forgiveness ritual I describe in Chapter ten.

Usually, the very thing that I need to do, the thing that would make a real difference, is the thing I am trying to avoid.

Funny isn't it?

They might not want you to either!

When you come from *Radical Self-Love*, you will begin to take care of yourself in ways that you may never have before. You may for example find yourself not wanting to gossip, or listen to gossip. You may begin to take time for yourself, to exercise, meditate, cook for yourself, to say no and mean it. I describe many powerful practices in the next chapter.

You may find that many people in your life are supportive of your self-care, and others not so much. Be grateful for the wise and supportive friends, teachers, mentors and family. They can remind you that you are a genuine *Radical Self-Love, Child of God*.

What about the *"not so much"* people?

People who are used to you coming from the victim identity may pull for you to go back to behaviors consistent with that identity. They may, for example, be accustomed to you providing unhealthy levels of support, or engaging with them in unhealthy behaviors.

Maybe you have been in the habit of always being available, always saying yes even when you want to say no. Maybe you've been financially supporting someone who you cannot afford to support, or who ought to be supporting him or herself. Maybe you have had a habit of complaining and gossiping. Maybe you have relationships that center around habitually binge eating or binge drinking.

It's not personal. It's not even that these people don't love you. They cannot give what they do not have. Bless them with your love. These relationships will either change or go.

People coming from a victim identity will simultaneously be attracted to and repelled by your *Radical Self-Love*. They will likely be jealous and may even be angry with you for taking care of yourself. What they really want is for you to take care of them. They will likely judge you, and may even say you are being selfish.

Bless their hearts. They just don't know any better.

Leave them alone. If they want to change, they will ask you for help. If they are willing, you can teach them to help themselves. If not, the best thing you can do is to be kind, pray for them, and wish them well. Some people just need a little more sleep. Let them sleep. That is the reason becoming conscious of your true identity is sometimes called a spiritual awakening. You are waking up to your *Radical Self-Love, Child of God true Identity*.

IS THIS A BOUNDARIES ISSUE?

Early on in this adventure to Radical Self-Love I did not have even a nodding acquaintance with the word *"no"* as a full sentence.

So when I first tried to *"Stop Being Stupid"* and love myself I believed it was necessary to have *"strong boundaries."* I believed I needed to learn how to protect myself. I believed I needed to figure out, and communicate to others what was acceptable and healthy for me. But, since I was still coming from the victim identity, I was not in the habit of being true to myself, because I didn't know what I was.

I believed others where doing things to me. I would establish these so called *"boundaries"* and just as quickly violate them myself, or allow others to violate them, or change my mind altogether. I was wishy washy at best.

This was especially true regarding men. I would tell a man I was starting to *"hang out with"* something like *"I don't have sex with a man unless I'm in a committed relationship."* I wanted to make sure he understood that I had a *"boundary"* about that. Then I would proceed to passionately make out with said man on successive evenings and within a week or two, I would have sex with him because he was persistent. I would then blame him for *"violating my boundaries."* Then I would get *"feelings"* for him. I would become emotionally attached to someone I barely knew. No wonder most of my relationships were volatile.

I'm going to say something potentially controversial. Boundaries are only necessary when you don't know that your authentic identity is *Radical Self-Love, a Child of God.* You are only concerned about boundaries when you are coming from a victim identity.

When you are coming from your *Radical Self-Love, Child of God Identity* your *"yes"* means yes and your *"no"* means no. You don't have a problem with yes or no, because either response comes from a place of love rather than fear. You automatically take good care of yourself, and simultaneously behave lovingly towards others.

As *Radical Self-Love, a Child of God* you know that when you are dealing with other people, you are always dealing with your brother or sister spiritually speaking. You practice patience and compassion rather than fear and anger when they come from a victim identity; when they engage in patterns of behavior that are usual, normal, and ordinary.

When their behavior upsets you, you take responsibility for your response, and do the necessary work to come back to your *Radical Self-Love, Child of God Identity.*

This does not mean that you condone destructive or inappropriate behavior in others, or have to be around it. If you determine that it is unhealthy or counter productive to be around them, then you stay away from them. You can love them, and pray for them without judgment or condemnation. You can love them from across town or across the country.

CHAPTER 9 SUMMARY

- Your personality is multi-faceted and although it is part of your self-expression, it is not your true identity.
- Adults who experience trauma as children usually have unresolved emotional trauma. That trauma resurfaces until it is resolved.
- As an adult you may try to separate from your child-self because you may blame the child-self for pain you experience.
- *"Inner Child"* work can help you resolve childhood emotional trauma.
- Purging and venting are tools to resolve emotional trauma and distinguish victim identity stories.
- Holding resentment or animosity towards others always produces suffering.
- Resentment is the result of a failure to accept life as it is or being unwilling to take a doable action.
- You are the one to "pay" or is penalized when you are unwilling to accept what is and forgive others and yourself.
- Judgment is always self-judgment.
- Examining resentment gives you access to hidden self-judgments, and thus is an access to freedom.
- Forgiving something does not mean condoning or liking something that you don't. Forgiving means you intend to be *Radical in your Self-Loving* and free, no matter what.
- Forgiveness is always self-forgiveness.
- To amend means to *put right, to change or modify for the better, to improve, to reform oneself.*
- Amends are generally advised if your behavior has been unloving, inconsiderate, unkind, overtly dishonest or inauthentic, which is also a form of dishonesty.
- Amends can be made directly to persons involved or indirectly by modifying your behavior.
- Direct amends usually involves acknowledging the harmful behavior and taking responsibility for the impact the behavior had on the other person.
- Indirect amends really means to live differently from the moment you take responsibility for the harmful behavior.

- The greatest living amends you can make is to consistently come from your authentic *Radical Self-Love, Child of God Identity*.
- You ego likes you to come from the victim identity. It wants the predictability, and therefore resists any transformation.
- Resistance is a sign that you are becoming aware. It is a sign that you are waking up; that you are making progress.
- You may experience resistant thoughts, emotions, or body sensations.
- Other people who are used to you playing the victim identity role may not want you to transform.
- Having *"boundary issues"* is a sign that you are coming from the victim identity.
- When you come from your authentic *Radical Self-Love, Child of God Identity* your *"yes"* means yes and your *"no"* means no.

Chapter 10
Are You Your Own Best Friend Yet?

"To keep a lamp burning, we have to keep putting oil in it."
– Mother Theresa

"You've got to know what you're really hungry for and eat that."
– Reverend Joanne Coleman

Every time I used to see old Jack, another of my loving and trusted mentors, he would say, *"Are you your own best friend yet?"* And I'd say, *"I'm working on it Jack, I'm working on it."*

I learned that my life really works when I act like I'm on my side; when I treat myself like I am my own best friend. I had to learn what that looked like. I didn't know. What do you do?

I had to learn how to nurture myself.

To **nurture** *means to nourish, educate, to further the development of, foster.*

To **nourish** *means to rear, to promote the growth, to furnish or sustain with nutriment, maintain, to support, to feed.*

Feed?

Ah ha! I understood. I was starving- starving for love, acceptance, peace, confidence, enjoyment, fun, kindness, support, and generosity. I hadn't eaten those things for myself very often. It was time to give to myself all of the things I was looking for others to give me.

It began to dawn on me that my life mattered to me. I mattered to me. I finally saw that I was enough. You are enough too.

While the morning and evening practices, and on-going training of your thinking are essential, more is needed. The following are some loving practices that are nurturing especially to the child-self.

I was out on my coffee walk one morning, and *God/Spirit* said to me clear as day, *"You cannot give what you do not live."*

"What's that supposed to mean?" I thought as I stomped home indignant! I complained to myself, *"Morning and night I've been doing my prayer and meditation, working really hard, being of service, doing all kinds of things, phew! I am exhausted!"*

What I realized was that I wasn't being kind and loving to me. I wasn't having much fun. I wasn't playing.

I got it. It was time to play, exult! Little Carol really needed to play!

To **exult** means *to leap up, to leap for joy, to feel great delight and be festive!*

It was time to feed my soul!

It's time for you to feed your soul!

RADICALLY SELF-LOVING PRACTICES

"To say Yes to life is at one and the same time to say Yes to oneself. Yes- even to that element in one which is most unwilling to let itself be transformed from a temptation into a strength."
– Dag Hammarskjold

"Take good care of yourself, nobody likes weak lemonade."
– Charles Singleton

Radical Self-Loving Practices include anything that up-lifts you mentally, emotionally, physically or spiritually.

The following loving practices are tools that support the body, mind and soul, and can foster your on-going growth and development in the art of *Radical Self-Love*.

I invite you to read through this section completely, and then go back and pick three practices to begin using immediately. Next, schedule time in your calendar to practice them.

I also suggest you ask someone to hold you accountable for fulfilling your intended practices. I find this especially useful when it comes to things like exercise. I work out with others. I find it almost impossible to talk myself out of a workout if I know someone else is depending on me too.

You may already do some of these practices, if so, bravo! And now I challenge you to add one or two additional practices. Use them *Radical Self-Love, Child of God*, you deserve the best!

Exercise

> "Move a muscle, change a state."
> – Tony Robins

Your body was designed to move. The emotional and physical benefits of exercise are irrefutable. Exercise strengthens muscles, bones, and circulation. It promotes the production of endorphins, your body's nature happy drugs and can foster a healthy sense of physical confidence. It is a tangible demonstration of *Radical Self-Love*.

When you are in a bit of a funk, just getting up off the couch and walking around the block can elevate your mood. Regular exercise three to four times a week is a critical component of maintaining your wellbeing.

Proper Nutrition

> "There is never enough of that which does not satisfy, you get fill-full-ment, instead of fulfillment."
> – Reverend Michael Bernard Beckwith

If I am feeding myself the thing I need physically, intellectually, emotionally, and spiritually, I do not engage in binge eating junk food. I eat nutritious meals and snacks.

What's interesting is that it goes both ways. Sometimes when I am feeling off, and I take the time to eat a really healthy meal, I feel better emotionally and become willing to do the spiritual work I need to do to get back in alignment.

On the other hand, if I am feeling off and I binge eat a bunch of junk food, I usually feel worse. I wasn't really hungry for that stuff. I was hungry for spiritual sustenance.

I don't beat myself up anymore when I do that kind of thing. I *"pump my breaks."* I simply get back to what works as soon as possible. Remember that deep practice is required to develop any new habit or skill.

Good Hygiene and Good Sleep Hygiene

Good physical hygiene is health promoting and just plain feels good. When I take the time to bathe, dress attractively and do my hair and make-up I feel better than when I don't, it's that simple, and it's fun for *"Little Carol!"*

Now what about sleep hygiene? Sleep hygiene is behavior that promotes restorative sleep. The first component is simply getting an appropriate amount of sleep. The second is to practice behaviors that ensure that you can fall asleep quickly and experience deep restful and rejuvenating sleep.

I have several suggestions around sleep hygiene. It is best to refrain from ingesting caffeine after about three in the afternoon. I suggest drinking a cup of herbal tea, or hot milk with a little honey just before bedtime.

I also recommend that at least one hour before sleeping you refrain from: working; exercising; listening to loud music; eating large meals; using computers or any other devices that produce light and are close to your face.

Long term insomnia, can be extremely detrimental if left untreated. There is ample research on sleep hygiene and even special therapists and doctors that can assist you if sleep is problematic. You are worth it.

Dating Yourself: Celebrate You!

"On the road of life, you have only one constant companion,
make sure you're good company for yourself.
– Robert Frost

One of the best practices I learned from the book *The Artist's Way* is to take yourself on dates.

I have been taking *"Little Carol"* on dates for years now, and she loves it! We go on hikes, to the movies, to coffee shops to read, to the Bead Store to make jewelry, get a pedicure, take walks, go for a fun bike ride or kayaks, explore unknown places, and go on adventures.

The structure is to spend at least an hour having fun, by yourself, and of course with your child-self. The intention is to embody the spirit of frolic, play and wonder. It is a form of celebration.

To **frolic** *is to be full of fun, to make merry, to play and run around happily, to romp.*

Romp *is to win easily!*

Wonder *is to cause astonishment, admiration, something awesomely mysterious or new to one's experience.*

To **celebrate** *is to demonstrate satisfaction by festivities or other deviation from routine, to honor.*

This is not a *"Ho hum I'm dating myself"* kind of thing. This is a *"let's see what we can get into today and have a romping good time!"* kind of party. It is a way to honor yourself by letting it rip!

I recently kayaked out to Four Mile Island in Priest Lake. I romped and frolicked around the perimeter of the Island. The Island is undeveloped, so there was no trail to follow, I had to find one. What a blast! It was so beautiful there and completely mysterious and awesome to see that I could, in fact, make it all the way around the island.

The important thing is to begin, and to continue. I started out with movies and bookstore. It took me time to develop a wider repertoire.

Spending time in Nature

> "In every wind that blows, in every night and day of the year, in every sign of the sky, in every blossoming and in every withering of the earth, there is a real coming of God to us if we will simply use our starved imagination to realize it."
> – Oswald Chambers

"Forget not that the earth delights to feel your bare feet and the winds long to play with your hair."
– Khalil Gibran

All of nature is on your side. All of nature can speak to you of the love, beauty and intelligence of *God/Spirit*. It is not oblivious to you. Spending time in nature is well, natural to us. We are part of it, and when we deliberately intend to connect, it feels wonderful.

Being in nature alone, without distraction, is critical. When you can see and hear and feel the beauty, love and support that is there in nature, it builds your capacity to experience it everywhere in your life.

Mother Nature is very nurturing to the soul. Spending even five minutes sinking your toes into the sand or grass, or simply gazing at the stars or the sky can soothe your soul.

Music and Art

There is music in your soul! Music is extremely empowering.

Listening to music, clapping to the beat, dancing and singing out loud empowers you because it lifts your vibration, and because when you move your muscles it facilitates the production of those wonderful endorphins.

Art and creativity are natural to you. Even in your darkest time, if you reflect, you may see that there was, even then, a creative genius in you.

That genius demands to be expressed. It may come in the form of cooking, painting, sculpting, working on engines, building things, making collages; it may be in writing, knitting, or drumming, taking photographs, drawing, whatever it is, do it!

Make it easy on yourself. Why not cooperate with it? It's got to come out anyways. Have fun! Make it light and allow it to flow through you. Boredom is a form of resistance and is the result, not the cause of blocked creativity.

Mirror Work

Mirror work means looking in a mirror and talking to yourself in a loving and empowering way. I couldn't do this at first. I'd look at my eyebrows instead because it was too uncomfortable to look directly into my own eyes. But I kept at it and gradually I could look myself in the eye and say *"I love you."* Mind you, I didn't mean it at first, but I do now.

Try it. Try it every time you go to the bathroom. Try it when you look in your rear view mirror. It is incredibly powerful.

Go try it right now. Find a mirror and look into your eyes and say *"I love you* _____ .(use your own name)

What was that like for you? If it was easy, you probably believe it. If it was hard, or if you couldn't do it at all, then this is a belief that is not active for you. Either way, deeply practicing this kind of Radical Self-Love can be very powerful if you are consistent.

I have discovered that when I look deeply into my own eyes, I can, if I stay with it, sense a loving Presence that I cannot describe. I experience peace, love, acceptance and support- what I have always wanted.

By the way, when you look deeply into anyone's eyes, you will find the same loving Presence looking back, you will find *Radical Self-Love, God/Spirits' Love.*

Self Hugging, and the Thymus Thump

I routinely wrap my arms around myself and say nice things like: *"You're doing good kid; I love you; I'm so proud of you."* "Little Carol" and all of the rest of me love this. It calms me down when I am anxious or agitated.

Another technique I learned in one of my teacher trainings is to use the thymus thump. The thymus gland is located beneath the breastbone and produces calming hormones. When the breastbone is tapped on, it stimulates the production of these hormones.

Thump, thump, thump your thymus and say something nice to yourself, like *"I love you honey."* This feels lovely! And oh by the way it works really well on dogs and cats to calm them down too!

EFT (Emotional Freedom Techniques)

Emotional or physical trauma can get *"stuck"* in the body and cause stagnation, pain and dysfunction. As my friend Mery (sic) would say, *"The issues are in the tissues.*" EFT is a tapping technique that can help release these trapped energies.

It involves tapping on various parts of the body while acknowledging the condition and then saying healing affirmations. It's similar to the thymus thump, only a bit more extensive in its scope. There are numerous books on EFT and many wonderful teachers of EFT, if you are interested in learning more.

I use EFT as part of my nightly forgiveness routine, tapping out resentment and tapping in love and forgiveness.

I have used the following exercise for over a decade to help work through physical pain, injury and illness. I have used it to facilitate movement through unproductive emotional states as well. I recommend that you do this once or twice a day.

This technique was given to me by one of my great teachers Marilyn Gordon. I reproduce it here with her permission.

Root Cause Technique

First identify the issue and get an intensity rating from 1-10: 1 being least intense and 10 being most intense.

Then, tap the SIDE OF THE HAND and say: "Even though I have this, _____, I deeply, completely love and accept myself." (Repeat this three times)

Now tap the following places and repeat the phrase three times::

1) EYEBROW (near the nose): "I am eliminating all the sadness in the deepest root causes of this _____."
2) UNDER EYE: "I am eliminating all the fear in the deepest root causes of this _____."
3) LITTLE FINGER (near the nail on the outside) "I am eliminating all the anger in the deepest root causes of this _____."
4) EYEBROW (outer edge): "I am eliminating all the emotional trauma in the deepest root causes of this _____."
5) UNDER THE MOUTH: "I am eliminating all the shame in the deepest root causes of this _____."
6) TOP OF THE HEAD: "I am eliminating all the guilt in the deepest root causes of this _____."

7) HEART: "I am eliminating all the grief in the deepest root causes of this _____."

8) INDEX FINGER (near the nail on the outside): "I forgive myself for ever taking this on. I love and accept myself. I was doing the best that I could. I don't need this _____ any longer, because I am now able to replace it with *Radical Self-Love* (or any other quality you choose). I let go of this _____. I have learned from this experience and now see it differently. (Here you can say anything that is healing and transformative.)

9) Check your intensity level, and repeat if you wish.

Laughter Makes for Good Medicine

If you don't have a sense of humor, you owe it to yourself to grow one. Laughter and light heartedness is extremely nurturing. Laughing causes your body to produce endorphins just like exercise- a great natural high.

Laughter causes a decrease in the production of the stress hormone cortisol, stimulates the immune system, and increases oxygen intake and heart rate.

So really, laughter is a great way to lower stress and get some exercise! One laughter researcher found that one-minute of laughter increased the heart rate in a manner equivalent to 10 minutes of working out on a rowing machine.

Watch funny movies. Do things that are goofy like skipping, whistling, playing games, or swinging on the park swings. I have never been able to stay grumpy while skipping, swinging, or whistling.

After all, you are the light of the world, so keep it light!

On-going Forgiveness Ritual. "Up until now..."

> "As I walked out the door toward the gate that would lead to my freedom, I knew that if I didn't leave my bitterness and hatred behind, I'd still be in prison."
> – Nelson Mandela

"Truth cannot deal with errors that you want."
– A Course in Miracles

"Behold, I make all things new!"
– Revelations 21:5

Sometimes I don't want to forgive. I savor being *"right"* or take a certain perverse pleasure in self-pity. When I notice I am rolling in that kind of victim-identity story about others or myself I use two very powerful tools taught to me by Reverend Maggie: the phrase *"Up until now..."*; and the self-healing techniques called Ho'oponopono.

Here's what I suggest, you say to yourself *"Up until now I've had the habit of thinking and believing _____ (state whatever description is appropriate) but now I choose to forgive."* After making that statement use the forgiveness ritual below.

Using the phrase *"Up until now..."* is a very gentle and *Radically Self-Loving* way of taking responsibility. This is really another way of using your dog training commands: drop it, leave it, come, stay and fetch. The additional specific component is the forgiveness piece.

The Hawaiian art of self-healing is called **Ho'oponopono**. It uses a forgiveness mantra that I have adopted. I repeat the mantra while doing the *"Thymus Thump,"* when I find myself feeling grumpy or judgmental of others or myself. It generally restores me to a sense of peace and balance.

The mantra is:

I love you.

I'm sorry.

Please forgive me.

Thank you.

There are books and websites devoted to this practice as a way of healing your life. I have found this practice to be immensely beneficial.

Forgiveness is a new beginning because it releases you from the past.

Close your eyes for a moment. Take three deep breaths and allow yourself to relax. Now allow yourself for just this moment to feel what it would feel like to be totally free. No one owes you anything, and you owe nothing. Just imagine it now. This is the power of forgiveness.

Peace is available when you demand nothing.

Forgiveness is your birthright *Radical Self-Love, Child of God*. Are you willing to receive your inheritance? It's waiting for you.

Hugging and Smiling

I smile often and hug anyone who is open to it. It feels great!

Smiling and hugging increases the production of endorphins, specifically the hormones serotonin and oxytocin the *"love hormones."*

Both smiling and hugging decreases the production of the stress hormone cortisol, and lowers both blood pressure and heart rate. Laughing, smiling and hugging are all linked to longevity.

Aside from the myriad health benefits, hugging and smiling feels good and emotionally connects us with others. There's no down side. Try it you'll like it!

Gratitude and Appreciation

"In all circumstances give thanks."
– 1 Thessalonians 5:18

The practice of gratitude and appreciation can change your life.

I practice gratitude and appreciation in several ways.

Gratitude Lists

I often write lists of things for which I am grateful. I find this especially helpful if I am indulging in self-pity. It seems to pop me out of that bog and back into my authentic self faster than anything else.

Appreciation Letters You Don't Have to Write

My parents taught me this concept. I write thank you notes and letters to people, and institutions expressing my appreciation for their excellence and/or kindness. I don't have to write these letters, I get to.

Acknowledging the contributions of others and expressing gratitude to them directly feels wonderful. It helps me to remember that everyone is always helpful and that everything is always supporting me.

Giving Thanks for Everything

This is an on going practice. It is beneficial to give thanks when things are going my way, and I do that- thanks for the beautiful sky! Gratitude keeps me connected to the source of my good.

Interestingly, I find expressing gratitude is even more powerful when circumstances are not to my liking. Expressing gratitude for the slow driver, the long line at the store or the spilled coffee can shift my view of the condition, and thus my experience.

For example, I had left my friend Debbie's apartment in Berkeley with just enough time to stop for coffee and make my ten am appointment. Not knowing the area well, I missed the turn to the coffee shop. My first reaction was to curse, but then I remembered to give thanks. I said *"thank you"* over and over as I went down to the next block, and doubled back. When I arrived at the shop there was a parking spot directly across the street; and there was still time on the meter! The funny thing was, that because I was practicing gratitude, I felt content and happy before I saw that there was convenient parking. It no longer mattered much. The parking spot was really just a bonus compared to the peace I obtained from being grateful.

Giving Thanks for Nothing

I find practicing gratitude for no thing, for nothing, is a powerful attractor. Remember we attract more of what we are. When I am grateful for no reason, for nothing, the law will either fill that void with something for which I can be grateful, or my view of things will change. What I had seen as a challenge or block, transforms into a blessing.

Praying for and with Others

It was suggested that I pray for other people, particularly if I resented them or had any kind of difficulty with them. I didn't like the idea at all. My initial response was *"Hell no! I'm not doing it!"* Once again, I took the long cut on this matter; perhaps you can be less stupid and obstinate.

What I have found is that if I pray for others I feel better, even good. I have found that if I persist, despite my initial resistance, I begin to mean what I pray. I have found that I begin to see even the most *"difficult"* people in a compassionate light, in a forgiving light. Most of the time praying daily for someone for a month will provide me access to compassion rather than the judgment I formally held. Try it.

Try it right now. Think of someone that you resent, or have judgment about. Try this simple prayer, *"Thank you God/Spirit for the gift of (say their name) in my life, thy will for (say their name). Help me to see (say their name) and myself as you see us. Thank you!"*

Yes, yes I know. I just snuck that forgiveness thing in again. Hey, it's really important. Keep it up, and I guarantee it will change you. It will free you.

I also routinely pray for my family, friends, co-workers, customers, mentors and the entire planet. It always leaves me feeling connected and grateful.

Now how about praying with other people. I was OK with reciting specific prayers in a large group setting like the *serenity prayer*; but I was wildly uncomfortable praying with other individuals or small groups, particularly if the prayer was *"off the cuff"* so to speak.

Prayer is such a personal thing, intimate. I felt embarrassed praying with others. It occurred to me like pooping in front of someone else; I just didn't feel at ease. Honestly, that was what it was like for me.

I did it anyway. I kept doing it despite the discomfort.

I now find praying with others to be powerful, intimate and incredibly humbling. It is especially powerful when I ask for someone to pray for me, or for a loved one. It almost always moves me to tears, and always leaves me feeling grateful and peaceful.

I invite you to try it for yourself.

CHAPTER 10 SUMMARY

- It is important to learn how to be your own best friend.
- Part of coming from your authentic *Radical Self-Love, Child of God Identity*, is nurturing yourself.
- Self-nurturing behaviors are those that feed the soul and are authentically *Radical Self-Loving*.

- *Radical Self-Loving* Practices include anything that up-lifts you mentally, emotionally, physically or spiritually.
- *Radical Self-Loving* Practices I recommend include:
  - Exercise
  - Proper Nutrition
  - Good Hygiene and Good Sleep Hygiene
  - Dating Yourself: Celebrating You!
  - Spending time in Nature
  - Music and Art
  - Mirror Work
  - Self Hugging, and the Thymus Thump
  - EFT (Emotional Freedom Techniques)
  - Laughter Makes for Good Medicine
  - On-going Forgiveness Ritual
  - Hugging and Smiling
  - Gratitude and Appreciation
    - Gratitude Lists
    - Appreciation Letters You Don't Have to Write
    - Giving Thanks for Everything
    - Giving Thanks for Nothing
- *Praying for and with others* is a powerful tool and often leads to an experience of deep connection with God/Spirit, others, and yourself.

Chapter 11
This is a good Beginning! Pay it Forward!

"A man wrapped up in himself makes a very small package."
– Ben Franklin

"God didn't make any mistakes or extra people."
– Reverend Michael Bernard Beckwith

"It's never too late to be who you might have been."
– George Elliot

The other morning on my coffee walk, God/Spirit ask two questions. "Now that you have your freedom, what are you going to do with it? And "What is worth sacrificing your life for?"

"Oh no you didn't!" I thought. *"Dang! Aren't I doing enough already?"*

Again the message was loud and clear- *"Calm your little ass down. You don't even know what sacrifice means. Quit fiddle fartin around."*

It's not like I hadn't heard this same thing a million billion times- my purpose is to be of service to *God/Spirit* and my fellows.

Right. So I looked up the definitions.

Sacrifice *means the destruction or surrender of something for the sake of something else, the act of offering to a Deity something precious.*

Precious *means something* of great value, highly esteemed or cherished.

Oh... And then it hit me- I am precious, and I am of great value. I am in fact, cherished by *God/Spirit*. The only thing that needs to be destroyed or surrendered is this victim identity, and these false beliefs. I must sacrifice those lies for the sake of my *Radical Self-Love, Child of God Identity*. I must sacrifice the victim identity to secure my freedom, and to help those I can serve.

When I am enthralled with the victim identity, I am not free. I must sacrifice that false identity to deliver my gifts as *Radical Self-Love, a Child of God*. My life is worth living when I do that. That is how I get to express being the very best me that I've ever been.

I now know that what is true for me is equally true for you. You also must be willing to sacrifice coming from the victim identity to deliver your gifts as *Radical Self-Love, a Child of God*.

You stand on the shoulders of your ancestors. They left you a rich material, mental and spiritual inheritance. They have done so much of the work for you. You don't think twice about going where you please with whomever you wish. You take for granted clean water, plentiful food, making phone calls, toasting toast, taking a hot shower, flying in airplanes, riding the bus, using the internet, worshiping as you see fit, or not at all.

You live like kings and queens of old. You do. You harvest what others have sown. Their prayers have been answered and you are living it. What is your part? What are you to share?

To **share** *is to partake of, use, experience or enjoy with others, to participate.*

You are meant to be a big person, with a big life making a big difference in the world. You are meant to share your gifts and to contribute in the way that only you can.

You may think it isn't possible for you. You may say, *"I'm only one person"*. Besides, you might say, *"I'm too old, too young, uneducated, too educated, too poor, blah, blah, blah."*

Come on now! Knock it off!

Everyone wants to contribute, to make a difference. You are one in 7.3 billion people on the planet, **AND YOU MATTER!**

There is something you are here to express in your unique fashion.

The universe is incomplete without you.

Yes, YOU!

So now that you know that, what are you going to do? Now that you know that you are *Radical Self-Love, a Child of God*, and that you have at your disposal an infinite supply, what are you going to do about it?

Really, what are you going to be about?

What's your unique purpose?

Only you can answer those questions.

It's OK if you don't have an immediate and clear picture of your exact life vision and purpose. If you are asking for clarity about your purpose, you will get it. It will take your deliberate choice, intention and attention to manifest it.

You did not come here just for you. You also came to serve others. You came here to make a difference for others. You have a responsibility to do what you came for.

You can begin right now to focus on the following purpose- *"I came here to make a difference for others. I am only here to be of service."*

When I first started this adventure, I was extremely self-conscious in social settings, especially when I didn't know very many people. My friend Motorcycle Doug use to coach me, *"Your only purpose in going to this function is to be of service. That may mean you simply listen to someone who needs to talk, or do the dishes."* It worked.

"I came to make a difference for others. I am only here to be of service." That continues to be one of my standard intentions throughout my day. It helps me to stay centered, present and free. It keeps me in acceptance.

Life is calling you out of the stands or off the sidelines, or off the banks of the river! Plunge in! Get in the game! Live! Celebrate! Play! Romp! Frolic! Explore! There is nothing to risk but boredom and misery.

You may say, **"but I have doubts!"**

So. So what!

As Reverend Sam Shoemaker advises, *"Act as if..."* or *"Fake it until you make it!"*

When I first consciously began this adventure, I said in a recovery meeting, *"Fuck faith, I need demonstrations of God/Spirit working in my life!"* If nothing else, I hope that story assures you that God/Spirit will meet you wherever you are and just loves you.

The truth was, I didn't have any faith at first. I needed to experience miraculous demonstrations of the care of *God/Spirit* in my life, consciously. I had to practice believing, acting as if, and then experiencing those demonstrations. That process translated into an undeniable faith and knowing that *God/Spirit* is working in my life at all times. That faith was one of *God/Spirit's* greatest gifts to me.

It's OK if you flit in and out of believing that you matter, and that you are wanted and needed and loved. Remember, as the Abrahams-Hicks say, "*A belief is just a thought you keep thinking,*" so it takes practice to believe in your heart that you are *Radical Self-Love, a Child of God,* and consistently operate from that belief.

So now what? Again, "*Act as if I am, and I will be.*" Regardless of your doubts, you may use your will power constructively to "*Act as if.*" I often use this powerful question: "If I knew, beyond a doubt that I was *Radical Self-Love, a Child of God,* what would I do in this situation?" and then I do that.

It's as if we all have access to an infinite number of Cosmic "*do-overs.*" You can start your day or your life over anytime you want to.

So what if you've made poor choices? So what if you have been coming from the victim identity your whole life? So what!

Big deal, join the rest of humanity. Look around your life, how many people do you know that are living up to their talents and potential?

As coach Mac on the show *Friday Night Lights* once yelled at his team that was screwing up royally and losing badly to a much less capable team **"You need to get your head out of your butt and play up to your potential!"**

I use that quote because I think it is hysterically funny, and because it makes a point. Now that you know the truth, it is your mandate to do the work so that you KNOW it in your heart and act on it, and then pay it forward.

You can choose to stand for others. You can stand in your own greatness, and stand for theirs.

The gig's up. I know who you are, and now so do you.

You can't pretend anymore.

Time to put your Big Girl and Big Boy panties on and get to work.

IT'S A WE-THING!

> "The pain you feel is the Love you withhold."
> – Nick Showers

> "There was the fullness of heaven and earth; the more that they
> gave to others, the more they had."
> – Kwang-Tze

To **serve** *is to be useful, to stand by, assist, attend, to answer the needs of, promote, to contribute, to benefit or help.*

You can serve up a helping of what's needed, wherever you go. It cost you nothing to smile, to let someone go ahead of you in traffic, to wave and smile rather than curse and give someone the middle finger. It cost you no money to listen with compassion or to express appreciation rather than be grouchy, to be loving and kind. It takes nothing from you to say thank you or I'm sorry.

OK, it does cost you something: You have to sacrifice the victim identity.

To serve up a helping of Love wherever you go and to whom-ever crosses your path is your natural activity. To come from your *Radical Self-Love, Child of God Identity* means you will be *Radically Loving* to others; you won't be able to help yourself. You will be like a flower that can't help but blossom.

Blooming and loving is natural to you. But unlike a rose that can't stop itself from blooming, you can stop yourself from being loving. Your blooming does require something. It requires your intention and your attention. You have to train yourself and that takes discipline.

You cannot fret, worry and regret and serve *God/Spirit* and your fellows at the same time. Who shall you serve? *Radical Love* or your trifling doubts, worries, judgments and petty manufacture slights.

ONWARD!

> "Discipline puts back in its' place that which ought to serve,
> but wants to rule."
> – Carthusus

"Mediocrity is self-inflicted and genius is self-bestowed."
– Walter Russell

"The surf that distresses the ordinary swimmer produces in the surf-rider the super-joy of going clean through it."
– Oswald Chambers

This is a never-ending adventure. Life continues to unfold. There is infinite possibility within you. You can be, do and have whatever you are willing to embody in consciousness. This kind of work makes it possible to choose how you will walk through life, rather than blithely accepting less than your own magnificence, your own genius. It is a ride! It is an adventure!

You are like a chick in an egg, or a butterfly in its' cocoon, you are growing into a world that you have never seen before, because you are a new creature now! Be firm yet gentle with yourself. You are in the process of becoming your greatest yet to be, again, and again and again.

COMMUNITY

"You will do foolish things, but do them with great enthusiasm."
– Good Earth Tea Bag Tag

"We're on a mission from God."
– Jake and Elwood Blues, The Blues Brothers screenplay
written by Aykroyd and Landis

Have you ever noticed that you are not alone here on planet earth?

Did it ever occur to you that you were meant to do this life thing WITH others?

There are communities galore. There are over one hundred 12-step groups, thousands of churches, temples, ashrams, Course in Miracle study groups, and Real Love support groups, etc. You can find a community if you seek it. I suggest you find a group or individuals who are doing this kind of work so that you can support each other.

It is not hard to do it by yourself; it's impossible. Independence is an illusion; try making your own oxygen.

It's a *"We Thing."* You are connected to others through bonds of affection and identity. If you are *Radical Self-Love, a Child of God*, and everyone else on the planet is too; then spiritually they are your brothers and sisters. We were made to be in communion with *God/Spirit* and with one another.

It is your spiritual mandate to love and be loved by others; and to serve and be served by others. That means that you must both give and receive. Try breathing by either only exhaling or only inhaling. It doesn't work. You must both inhale and exhale to live. You must both receive and give for your life to work.

When you allow others to be of service to you, you allow them to contribute. You receive and so do they. When you contribute to others, you receive as well. It is the Law. Besides, it is a satisfying, fulfilling, beautiful, and meaningful way to live! You are worth the effort!

A world that works for everyone is possible. We can do together, with the power of *Radical Love*, what we could not do alone. Besides God/Spirit is right here with us. And if God/Spirit is for us there can be nothing against us.

Let's make the difference we were meant to make!

Begin now!

I love you my brothers and sisters! Thank you for loving me!

Carol Wirth

Chapter 11 Summary

- You have a purpose and you matter.
- Your purpose is to be of service to *God/Spirit* and others.
- You must sacrifice the false-victim identity to be free to deliver your gifts as *Radical Self-Love, a Child of God*.
- You have inherited a rich world from our ancestors.
- You are meant to share your gifts- to contribute in the way that only you can.
- You came here to make a difference for others. You have a responsibility to do what you came for.
- Try adopting the purpose- *"I came here to make a difference for others. I am here to be of service."*

- So what if you have doubts! *God/Spirit* meets you where you are.
- Regardless of your doubts, you may use your will power constructively to *"Act as if."*
- To serve up a helping of Love wherever you go and to whom-ever crosses your path is your natural activity.
- This is a never-ending adventure. Life continues to unfold. There is infinite possibility within you.
- It not hard to do it by yourself, it's impossible. Independence is an illusion.
- It is your spiritual mandate to love and be loved by others; and to serve and be served by others.

About the Author

Carol Wirth has been a spiritual mentor/teacher for the past 20 years. Stop Being Stupid is her first solo book.

Carol uses her life as a teaching tool in this transformational guidebook to the adventure of your own personal realization and embodiment of Radical Self-Love.

Carol grew up in rural eastern Washington State, but spent most of her adult life in the East Bay Area of California. She was, for 26 years, a math and science teacher and high school administrator in Oakland, California and Spokane, Washington.

She has developed and led spiritual retreats, as well as trained and supervised an inner city youth peer conflict resolution team. She was an Introduction Leader for Landmark Education for three years.

Her interest and hobbies include photography, piano, cooking, reading, watercolor painting, weight lifting, running, basketball, amateur and professional boxing, rock climbing, stock market investing and stock trading, and she is a football and music enthusiast.

She currently resides in Spokane, Washington where she continues her work as a spiritual mentor/teacher, writer, and part-time Barista at Starbucks.

READING GROUP GUIDE

Questions and Topics For Discussion

1) How is being victimized different from engaging in the victim identity?
2) Is a tiny *"drop of sewage"* acceptable in your life?
3) What is it like to be around someone who is coming from the victim identity?
4) What circumstances most contribute to you adopting the victim identity?
5) What aspect of your life is being adversely affected by engaging in the victim identity?
6) What benefits do you get out of believing you are the victim identity?
7) How is blaming and complaining detrimental?
8) How do your habits determine your life experience?
9) What is the benefit of taking complete responsibility for your life?
10) What victim-identity patterns do you engage in?
11) How are choice and awareness connected?
12) What is meant by the phrase *"new view, new you"*?
13) Why is acceptance a powerful tool to deal with upsetting life events?
14) How does Radically Loving yourself benefit the entire world?
15) In what way is a "normal" life inconsistent with choosing your authentic *Radical Self-Love, Child of God Identity?*
16) What role does cultivating a relationship with *God/Spirit* play in Radically Loving yourself?
17) What is the relationship between beliefs, habits and affirmations?
18) What is your personal experience when you keep or honor your word? And when you don't?
19) According to spiritual law, why are beliefs the driving force of your life? Give an example from your own life.
20) Discuss the following statement. *Spiritual law creates justice without judgment.*
21) In what way are seemingly "dark times" beneficial?
22) In what way is deep practice necessary in creating new habits of thought?
23) What is the point of a morning and evening spiritual practice?
24) For what reason is it critical to exert dominion over your attention?

25) What are the best ways to utilize the "dog training" commands to train your thinking?

26) In what way is *Inner Child* work an important part of Radical Self-Love?

27) Discuss the relationship between judgment, resentment, forgiveness and freedom.

28) How does purging differ from venting and how could they benefit you?

29) In what way are amends an important part of Radical Self-Love?

30) What are the types of resistance you experience within yourself? And from other people?

31) What are three new self-nurturing practices you are willing to take on?

32) What would life be like if you were being your authentic best?

33) What gifts do you have to give?

34) What is meant by the phrase, "Independence is an illusion"? And, how do you deal with what you believe it means?

Made in the USA
San Bernardino, CA
24 June 2016